CHATS ON VIOLINS

BY

OLGA RACSTER

SECOND IMPRESSION

LONDON

T. WERNER LAURIE

To
CICELY R. TRASK

CONTENTS

CHATS ON VIOLINS

—•◇•—

INTRODUCTION

MANY people are inclined, I believe, to accept the violin as an instrument apart from others, and rather resent the idea of its reaching perfection through imitation. I do not wish for a moment to shake the faith of those who hold this, or any other opinion (and I think the history of the violin is vague enough to admit any number), I simply intend to strive to follow in the steps of the great George Washington by telling as few lies as I can.

To begin with, there is little doubt that the violin *has* reached its present perfection through imitation, or I may say heredity. Nothing seems to have been discovered which tends to point to the

A

violin as the invention of any one man;
rather it appears to be the result of a
collection of inventions which ingenious
men have made in different centuries. For
instance, from the primitive twang of the
hunting-bow came the first suggestion of
a musical sound produced by a vibratory
string. From Mercurie's invention of the
Lyre played with a plectrum (bow) came
the first idea of three or more strings on
one instrument. From the monochord
invented in the third century by Claudes
Ptolemeus, came the first idea of a peg by
which to regulate the tension of a string;
from the Rebec, six centuries later, came
the first idea of a finger-board, and the
foundation of the pitch of the first three
strings of the fiddle. From the Crouth
came the first idea of ribs to join the
belly and back. Through the ancient
custom of holding bow-instruments between
the knees came the gradual inward curving
of the ribs. Finally, from the early Viols,
which first appeared in the fifteenth century
in Germany, came the crude outline of the
violin. Very bulky and heavy looking were
these early Viols, and terribly uncomfortable
to play on; yet one can distinctly trace in

them a noble struggle towards the graceful curves of the perfect Stradivarius form.

The written history of the evolution of the violin is a very short one, but in reality it occupied about eight hundred years, and wonderful to relate, having once reached perfection, it has remained untouched by the progress which surrounds it. For three hundred years the violin has kept its present model, and attempted innovations have only proved that the task of alteration is as difficult and unavailing as improving Cologne Cathedral or remodelling a Greek statue.

THE FIDDLE'S ANCESTORS

.

CHAT I

THE FIDDLE'S ANCESTORS

ITS ORIGIN, AS DESCRIBED IN MYTH, TRADITION, AND FANCY

THE story of the creation of the Greek "Lyre," which by some authorities is accepted as the founder of all bow instruments, is told by the Greek mythologist, Appolodorus, who says it was invented in the year of the world 2000.

According to him, the god Mercury constructed the lyre from the shell of a dead tortoise, which he discovered lying high and dry on the banks of the Nile. Only the nerves and sinews were left stiff and distended within the shell, and the god accidentally touching the tortoise with his foot, caused these to vibrate. Liking the sound produced, he raised the shell, and hollowing it, strung it

7

with three strings. The story gracefully
continues that he dedicated each string to
one of the three Greek seasons—the highest
to spring, the middle to summer, and the
lowest to winter.

Pausanias also attributes the invention of
the Lyre to Mercury, but states that Mercury
found the dead tortoise in an Arcadian
mountain called Chelydorea, near Mount
Cyllene.

Tradition tells us that the first of all bow
instruments was invented about five thousand
years ago by Ravanon, a mighty King of
Ceylon. From its description, this primitive
fiddle was quite an advanced affair, being
strung with the intestines of wild beasts, and
played with a haired bow. It was christened
"Ravanostron," after the inventor's name,
and is in use amongst the Hindoos at the
present day.

Jean Rousseau, a quaint French writer of
the seventeenth century, is of opinion that
Adam, through his early connection with
Paradise, transmitted the idea of a fiddle to his
children. He says it is easy to understand
why Adam did not make a fiddle in Paradise;
of course, had he wished he could easily have
done so, but in that terrestrial region he was

so surrounded with beautiful and delicious things, that any invention of science or art would have diminished, instead of augmented, these charms ; and after his fall, he was too sad and hopeless to think of any kind of diversion to lighten his miseries. With Adam's children it was different : they had never known a Paradise to regret, nor felt the disgrace of expulsion, so they were ready and willing to invent for themselves a small Paradise in the shape of a fiddle.

Jean Rousseau's intense love of the viol, of which he was a distinguished professor, probably led him to devise the foregoing delightful story.

The Rebec.

The rebec, I am sorry to say, had nothing of the Vere de Vere about it. A common, loud, harsh, little thing, it mixed with common, loud, harsh people. Nobody admired it, nobody loved it; like the ugly duckling it was looked upon with disfavour, and snubbed on every opportunity.

Originally Arabian it was brought into Spain by the Moors in the eighth century. From thence it passed into Italy, and it is not improbable that the eventful reign of Charlemagne scattered it amongst many nations.

It seems almost incredible that such a much abused instrument should have been so popular, and have lasted through nearly five centuries, even longer; for when viols first began to be heard of a century later, this "rolling stone" of the violin family was still bobbing about.

Perhaps it was a case of the survival of the fittest, and the little Rebec being strongly made and portable, could be used in a variety of useful ways:—In self-defence, or as a footstool, a poker, a mask before the face; and when it came to pieces its rotund little body might have formed a capital drinking bowl or saucepan.

Be this as it may, those historic minstrels, the Troubadours and Jongleurs welcomed it; it was so small and portable, so easily tucked away under their great cloaks, and with the addition of a harp, little more could be wanted to charm their patrons.

From one noble mansion to another these minstrels would roam, wedding music and words in wild song, and wiling away many an hour for the squire, the warrior, and the wife who watched for her lord's return from the wars.

In those primitive days, how welcome must the minstrels have been, and how wonderful and versatile their powers to amuse! Probably their entertainment would open with a dance played on the little rebec, then a story of romance, or a thrilling tale of the bravery of Charlemagne or some popular hero ; perhaps after this the Sautiére would be danced in couples, or the Corrente in rounds, the minstrels playing and singing at the same time :

> " Qui sont-il, les gens qui sont riches?
> Sont-il plus que moi qui n'ai rien ?
> Je cours je vas, je vir', je viens
> J'ai pas peur de perd ma fortune.
> Je cours je vas, je vir', je viens
> J'ai pas peur de perde mon bien."

Or perhaps a love ditty :

> " Si j'étais petit oiseau
> Si J'avais deux petites ailes
> Je volerais vers toi."

When the entertainment was ended, the minstrels would receive some small reward, sometimes money, frequently just bed and board. According to a contemporary ditty

of John le Chaplain, the latter was a very
customary form of payment :

> "In Normandy a song or tale
> Is current coin for wine or ale,
> Nor does the friendly host require
> For bed or board a better hire."

Alas! poor minstrels they were not
always even as fortunate as this, sometimes
they played, and played, and played, and like
poor Colin Musét received no reward whatever.   This minstrel who was one of the
best French writers of the thirteenth century
bitterly complains of the want of consideration shown him by a great Baron to whom
he had played at his hotel. He says he
received nothing in return, not even his
wages, and sadly laments being compelled
to return to his wife with empty pockets,
because she scolded him so, and only received
him with caresses when he succeeded in
obtaining a good round sum. But of all
ministrelsy, the woman minstrel was the
worst rewarded.   In Henry VIII.'s privy
purse expenses relating to music, two signi-
ficant items run thus:

> "For playing of the Morris Daunce   £2 o o
> *To a woman that singeth with a Fiddell* o 2 o"

Although there is not much that is respectable in the history of the Rebec, still I must admit that he had some feathers in his mythical cap: Charles VIII. mentions giving a fee to Raymond Mounet, "*Jouer de Rebec*," and in 1523 there existed a "*Jouer ordinare de Rebec du Roi*." Henry VIII., whose matrimonial complications did not preclude him from being an ardent flute player, included three rebecs in his State band, and in his privy purse expenses of 1531, quotes "20s. paiede for a Rebecke." Chaucer mentions the rebec most politely in his description of the parish clerk:

> "In twenty manners could he trip and daunce
> After the schoole of Oxenforde tho'
> And with his legs casten to and fro,
> And play songs on a small *Ribible*."

The literature of the day, however, was not always as kind as this in its criticisms of the rebec. A Spanish poet called it the "squalling rebec," and a French poet who was evidently not an admirer of the fair sex said: "Its tone emulated the female voice."

In Paris free use was made of the poor rebec's name for every kind of ridicule;

and in London, where all sorts of stringed instruments were generously dubbed "fiddles," the rebec found small favour. In truth neither fiddlers or fiddles were looked upon as anything more than beggars and noise. Gosson writing in the time of Queen Elizabeth gives a good idea of the low esteem in which fiddlers were held. He says:

"London is so full of unprofitable pipers and fiddlers, that a man can no sooner enter a tavern than two or three cast of them hang at his heels to give him a daunce before he departs."

When I read this paragraph of Gosson's, I can always conjure a picture for myself of those humble, shabby fiddlers asking the favour of playing you a dance on their scrubby little rebec. Poor, cold, sometimes starving figures they look, but bravely and unconsciously laying the foundation stone of the future Antonius Stradivarius.

In 1628 the contempt and disgust for the rebec became aggressive; turned away here, kicked out there, the doom of this poor little instrument was finally sealed by the Civil Lieutenant of Paris. This gentleman issued an order which forbade any other instrument save the rebec to be played in taverns and low places. And thus when the star of the real violin was just preparing to rise, its humble relation, the rebec, was voted an outcast and hopelessly doomed for the rest of its life.

Few, if any, authentic specimens of this instrument now exist, but numerous representations of its original form are to be found in the pictorial representations of thirteenth century painters. During a recent visit abroad, I came across many such pictures in the ancient cathedrals and churches, and, oh! irony of fate! the rebecs were all in the hands of sweet little angels who seemed not at all disconcerted by clasping such a disreputable little person as Monsieur Rebec.

As a fitting end, I may say with Scott (*The rebec went*):

"To the wild dust from whence he sprung,
Unwept, unhonoured, and unsung."

Description of the Rebec.

In shape it somewhat resembled a mandoline. It was played with a bow, and the player rested the instrument against the left breast. The three strings were of stout gut, and the tuning was the same as the three lower strings of the violin.

The Rebec's Name in Different Countries.

SPANISH   .   . Rabil.
PORTUGUESE   . Rabel, Rabil, Anabel.
ITALIAN   .   . Rìbeba, Ribeca.
FRENCH   .   . Rebec, Ribèbe.
GERMAN   .   . Giege.
ENGLISH   .   . Rebec, Ribible, Fydell.

The Crouth.

The crouth, crwth, crowth, or crowd, as it is variously spelt, was contemporary with the little rebec. It is usually attributed a Welsh origin, and in one sense its career was somewhat like the rebecs, for it shared with the harp (the Welsh "Wood of Joy") the honour of accompanying the songs of the Bards.

Its great age is verified by the distinct mention made of it by a Welsh king who reigned from 904 to 948. This monarch

chronicles giving as reward a present each
to three Bards :

To the first : a harp.

To the second : a crouth.

To the third : a cornemuse (bagpipe).

I cannot say of the crouth that it was
tucked away under the cloaks of the
minstrels, for it does not look a tuckable
contrivance.   There is a square, gauche
expression about it that suggests angular
dancing and hard rhymes. Unconsciously
I have always classified it as an instrument
for mounted minstrels who must possess
square faces, and ride on nice, fat, hard
horses.   Their dress I am sure would be
of leather, and they would proceed from
house to house, sedately and heavily with
the crouth firmly strapped on their backs.

Neither great abuse nor great praise seems
to have been its lot ; it never even reached
the rebec's glorious dispraise.   It seems
to have been just the crouth, a square
person with a very unyielding face : the
Puritan of the Violin family.

I think it must have moved in rather
better circles than the rebec, for only once
in the time of Henry VIII. do I find it in
any sort of trouble.   Even then it is nothing

B

very much, only a certain John Hogan is
informed against for singing with a "crouth
or fydell." And again of this one cannot
be quite certain, for instruments have been
so miscalled that the crouth above mentioned might have been "*little rebec*" after all.

A present of a crouth was made to the
Antiquarian Society of London in 1775;
judging from its description, the effects it
produced must have been extremely dull.
The bridge being flat, the strings were
necessarily vibrated at one and the same
time, thus producing a continuous succession
of chords. Added to this, the bow is
mentioned as "awkward and heavy."

Messrs Sandys & Foster, in their book,
give a picture of a crouth the property of
C. W. G. Wynne, Esq. It is described as
worm-eaten, and of a greater age than the
ticket within. The ticket runs thus:

maid in the paris of
Anirhengel by Richard
Evans Instruments maker
In year 1742.

But one of the most interesting contribu-
tions to the history of the crouth is the
discovery made by Mr Edward Heron-Allen

of a document signed and sealed by " Roger
Wade, the Crowder," in 1316. This deed
lies in the muniment room in Berkley Castle,
Gloucestershire, the seat of the Barons
Fitzhardinge, and its seal undoubtedly gives
a correct delineation of the instrument.
Owing to the courtesy of Mr Heron-Allen,
I am able to append the document rendered
from mediæval French into English, and
also to reproduce a representation of the
seal.

The bond reads as follows :

" To all who shall see or shall hear this
letter, Roger Wade, crowd-player (sends)
salutations in (the name of) God. Whereas
Warren de l'Isle is bound and indebted to
me in (the sum of) one hundred and twenty
pounds sterling, to be paid and returned at
the Feast of Pentecost next to come after
the date of this letter, as is also more fully
set forth in a letter of obligation which the
same Warren has to (testify) this fact to me,
sealed with his seal. I, the before-named
Roger, will and grant for myself, for my
heirs and for my executors, that if the
before-named Warren, his heirs or his
executors, pay and return to me, to my

heirs or to my executors, or to my ascertained attorney, at the said Feast of Pentecost next to come, sixty-nine pounds four shillings and one penny sterling, that thenceforward the before-named Warren, his heirs and his executors, shall be acquitted and discharged from the whole of the said debt of one hundred and twenty pounds for ever, and that from that hour forward the said letter of obligation, made at the same (time as) the debt, shall be cancelled, broken, and nullified, and held for nothing in the future. But if the before-named Warren, his heirs and his executors, make default in paying to me, to my heirs, or to my executors, or to my ascertained attorney, the before-mentioned sixty-nine pounds four shillings and one penny sterling, at the term above mentioned, thenceforward shall remain and must remain to me, to my heirs, and to my executors, our whole and undamaged (right of) action to demand and recover against the before-mentioned Warren, against his heirs and against his executors, the whole of the said debt of one hundred and twenty pounds according to the form of the said letter of obligation, without any contradiction. In witness of which thing

I have placed my seal to this letter. Given at London the Sunday next after the Feast of St Bartholomew the Apostle, in the tenth year of the reign (of) the King Edward, son (of) the King Edward."

Warren de l'Isle above mentioned was a person of considerable importance. His correct title was "Warine de'l Isle, Baron d'Isle," and he was a direct descendant of Warine Fitzgerald, who was in the Scottish wars in the time of Edward I., and later became "Governor of Windsor Castle and Warden of the Forest." Subsequently he joined Thomas, Earl of Lancaster, against the Spencers in 1320-21, and, being taken prisoner, was hanged at York with Lord Mowbray. His great grand-daughter and only surviving descendant married Thomas, Lord Berkeley, ancestor of the Barons Fitzhardinge.

A Welsh player of the crouth, by name John Morgan, was living in the island of Anglesey as late as 1853, he was then sixty years of age, and in all probability was the oldest and last of the crouth players. I say with confidence the *last*, because he does not seem to have imparted his know-

ledge to the younger generation, for at the
present day both the instrument and method
are quite extinct.

Description of the Crouth.

In its earliest form the crouth carried only
three strings ; the later carried six.

Of the ancient and earliest form used by
the Bards all trace is lost. The tuning of
the six-stringed crouth was thus :

Four of these strings were stretched over
the finger-board, and two were stretched off
the finger-board, at the side to be plucked
by the thumb of the left hand, as required.
The sound-holes were perfectly round, and
one of the legs of the bridge passed through
the sound-hole and rested on the back of
the instrument, thus acting as a sound-post.

The Vielle or Hurdy-Gurdy.

While that pious French King Louis IX.
was preparing for the Crusades, and poor

weak Henry III. of England was squandering money in fruitless wars, the troubadours were advancing things artistic by creating enthusiasm for their literature and music. No longer looked upon as beggars, these wanderers were welcomed as honoured guests, and were handsomely rewarded. They were now constantly attached permanently to the different Courts, and it was the custom to shower on them the most costly gifts of robes and vestments :

> "And all these costly robes of state
> In all three hundred and thirty-eight,
> To fiddlers and buffoons given."

Ever advancing, it was in the minstrel's hands that each successive instrument found trial and favour, and thus it was with them that the new French instrument called the vielle first found its home.

This gay and afterwards fashionable little contrivance of the thirteenth century is considered to be a development of our friend the crouth. One cannot truthfully say that the resemblance between them is striking, for this brilliant child of a commonplace parent seems to have striven to obliterate any family likeness. It preserved the faintest outline of

the crouth, but it flung off the surrounding
frame, the hard outline, the name, the manner
of playing, the dull quality of tone, and
finally tripped off with the addition of gay
ribbons, scarcely to be recognised as remotely
connected with Puritanical Mrs Crouth.

I have always erroneously thought of the
hurdy-gurdy as an instrument confined to
the use of beggars, because my childhood
memories picture many a vision of the
ragged little Savoyards, with their monkey
and hurdy-gurdy.

Even now that the history of musical
instruments informs me of my mistake, I
find it difficult to disconnect the hurdy-
gurdy from the beggar boy, the monkey,
and the picturesque rags. In justice to the
vielle I must say that the ragged stage
was only the first and the last, and, had I
been able to stretch my life backwards as
far as the eighteenth century I should have
been rewarded by seeing the vielle in all its
glory; the Court instrument *par excellence.*

The man who was responsible for the
vielle's rise in life, was a Parisian musical
instrument maker named Bérton, who
flourished about 1716. Ingenuously this
man took the bodies of ancient lutes,

rebecs, and theorbos; and used them for the bodies of his vielles, thus marvellously improving the quality of tone. With the wisdom of Satan he ornamented them profusely, and gave their outline more grace than previously. Rendered so tempting looking, Society soon became attracted, and Society beauties did not hesitate to attach this dainty toy round their necks with gay ribbons. For did it not show the elegant figure, the rounded arm, the graceful turn of the wrist, and the coquettish bend of the head? And, was it not most flattering and delightful to play such charming pieces as "La Galante," "La Sensible," "La Passioné," and other dainty bits dedicated to them by their admirers?

When one reflects how great a part vanity plays in life, one cannot be surprised at the quick manner the vielle sailed into favour.

"Madame," says the music master, "theorbos, rebecs, and lutes are out of fashion; at Court the only instrument is the vielle;" and Madame anxious to copy *les dames de la Coure* hastens to learn the vielle. Next, Madame's friends becoming secretly envious of her graceful pose, also

acquire the art of the vielle, and *hey presto*!
'tis all the fashion.

Beside the many amateurs of this instrument there were also professional artists
who gained great reputations.   Two notable
virtuosi were Laroze and Janot, and a woman
player called Fanchon reached a high pinnacle of fame which she was unfortunately
unable to keep owing to her degraded tastes.
A very successful play was written about her
called "*Fanchon la Vielleuse.*"   In this the
heroine, unlike the living Fanchon, was a
highly virtuous girl who played the vielle,
and married a delightful colonel.

In 1773 a further development of the
vielle was made by Louvet, who was a
professor of the instrument.   He constructed
a vielle which he strung with twelve metal
strings, and called it the violin-vielle.   But
long before this the vielle was back in the
hands of beggars and Savoyard boys, and
neither love nor science could save it or bring
it back to its former grandeur.   Plenty of
hurdy-gurdys still exist and some of the
very small ones are most beautifully
ornamented, but the tone is so scratchy and
noisy that no ears accustomed to the sound
of a fiddle can listen to it with any pleasure.

*The Vielle or Hurdy-Gurdy of
Madame Adelaide.*

Louis XV.'s eldest daughter, Madame Adelaide was gifted with such an immoderate desire for learning of every description that her knowledge became wide and varied. She studied history, she studied ancient languages, she studied chemistry, physics and geology, and, still not content, perfected herself in the playing of every kind of instrument.

From the Jew's harp to the hunting horn (which she played to such perfection as to render the *picqueurs de la Grande Ecurie* jealous), there was none she did not know. Amongst them all, however, there was one she loved best—the vielle.

Being her boon companion in many a lonely hour, she became one of the most proficient players of her day, and even the celebrated *veilleur*, Danguy, was most proud of the perfection attained by his distinguished pupil.

Of the rest of the Royal family Madame Adelaide saw but little ; she and her sisters occupied the whole of one side of the Château de Versailles, and only once each morning did their father honour them with a short

visit before starting for his favourite
chasse.

On 14th March 1764, the princess had
awaited her father's visit in vain, and hearing
the preparations for the hunt in the courtyard without concluded the paternal visit
would not take place that morning. Sitting
by her fire with her beloved vielle on her
knee, she was occupying herself by de-
ciphering a new piece of music written for
the vielle by Batinsson, when her Royal
father suddenly entered bearing in his hand
a silver mug of coffee which he dearly loved
making himself. Placing the *cafetière*
carefully on the hot coals, he buried himself
amongst the cushions of a comfortable easy
chair, the luxury of which he always greatly
enjoyed. As soon as he was seated, Madame
Adelaide placed a small round table of
Japanese lacquer by him, and put her
precious vielle on the tray which contained
her father's cup. Then she rang a bell to
inform Madame Victoire, in her apartments,
of the paternal visit. Madame Victoire rang
up Madame Sophie, and Madame Sophie in
her turn rang up Madame Louise, who was
the most isolated.

Poor little deformed Madame Louise did

not expect the king's visit, and was quite
unprepared to attend. Thinking the hour for
his appearance past she had thrown of the
heavy habiliments prescribed by Court
etiquette. The moment she heard the tinkle
of the bell she hurriedly donned a huge
crinoline and covered it with a heavy and
ample skirt, profusely embroidered. These
in the uttermost haste she attached round
her thin little waist, and to hide the *néglige*
of the rest of her toilette she threw a long
black silk mantle over her shoulders. But
even these preparations took some time, and
the hasty king, momentarily growing impatient, restlessly glanced out of the window,
and with a sudden movement of anger, upset
the round table, the vielle, the cup, and
strode out of the room and out of the château
minus his coffee. Poor Madame Adelaide
remained gazing at the fragments, and, with
tears in her eyes, gently stooped and gathered
her broken vielle.

A few days after this episode, the princess
received a visit from Danican Phylidor, a
distinguished Court musician. He brought
with him a superb vielle—a present from
Louis XV. to his daughter—and the following little note:

"MY DAUGHTER,—I send you an instrument to replace the one I broke; keep it always. May it recall to you the effects of my foolish impatience, and may this souvenir help to mend the impetuousness of your character."

Madame Adelaide cherished this vielle with great care; she took it with her to her apartments in the Château de Bellevue, where it hung suspended on the wall of her room. Only when she left France in 1791, was she forced to leave it behind with all her furniture.

During the terrible pillage of 13th July, it was looted by the people, and after many vicissitudes eventually came into the hands of Monsieur Colin, a French *luthier*.

Monsieur Colin took great care of the instrument, and never approached it but with the greatest respect. It is said that he remarked that this vielle, without being touched, often gave out sad wails like that of an æolian harp, and that this coincidence always preceded some sad event in the Royal family. One Sunday Monsieur Colin was about to sit down to dinner when he was startled by a dismal wail, long and

pronounced. He rushed into the shop
and found the noise was caused by the
simultaneous breaking of all the strings
of the vielle. Immediately he felt convinced
that some great misfortune had occurred
to the Bourbon family. A few days later the
papers announced the death of Madame
Adelaide, 18th February 1800, the exact
day the vielle's strings snapped. This
instrument now lies in the Musée Instru-
mental of the Paris Conservatoire.

Description of the Vielle or Hurdy-Gurdy.

The earliest form had six strings extend-
ing in pitch from the low G of the fiddle
to the G two octaves above. Four of the
strings passed over the bridge and finger-
board, and two lay at the side giving out
a continuous bass, which had a 'bagpipe
effect. In France these two strings were
called "Les Mouches," and in England
"Drones." To soften the harsh tone of these
two strings, fine cotton was often wound
round the part touched by the revolving
wheel. Over the finger-board lay a sort of
key-board and keys which were pressed by
the fingers to make the notes on the strings

Pepys gives an amusing description of the instrument as follows:

"To the Musique-meeting at the Post-office, where I was once before. And thither anon came all the Gresham College, and a great deal of noble company: and the new instrument was brought, called the arched viall, where being tuned with lute-strings, and played on with kees like an organ, a piece of parchment is always kept moving; and, the strings which by the kees are pressed down upon it, are grated in imitation of a bow by the parchment; and so it is intended to resemble several vialls played on with one bow, but so basely and so harshly, that it will never do."

PEPYS, 5*th October* 1664.

VIOLS AND EARLY VIOLINS

c

CHAT II.

I THINK it must have been a desire to imitate the singing voice which suggested the innovations and experiments made on the violin's ancestors towards the middle of the fifteenth century.

Musical instrument makers became suddenly eager to contrive something which would give a sweeter and more musical sound than that produced by any of the existing stringed instruments. The preliminary step was taken when the Hurdy - Gurdy became a bow instrument with the name of Vielle à Archet. Then came attempts to obtain greater resonance : the position of the sound-hole was altered, also the shape of the back and belly, and a more graceful outline attempted. As the result of this ingenuity and research, the world of music was pre-

35

sented with a bunch of instruments called
Viols, which bore some resemblance to the
recognised fiddle form.

Big and little, these viols emerged from
the workshops of Jean Ott and Hans Frey
in Nuremburg, from Joan Kerlino in Brescier,
Guerson in France, and Bolles and Rosse in
England. Big and little, they crept into the
favour of musical amateurs ; and soon old
and young periwigs showed a decided
preference for nodding over Viols instead of
joining in madrigals.

Presently Viol parties became favourite
entertainments, and Mr Periwig took as
much delight in inviting Monsieur Perreuque
to join in his concert of Viols on such and
such a day and hour as he had formerly
experienced in asking him to his madrigal
parties.

Truth to tell the advent of the Viol seemed
to take away the zest for singing madrigals.
Perhaps people were weary of striving to
sing in tune, perhaps the new Viol music
threw the charms of the madrigal into the
shade ; whatever may have been the reason,
it is certain that after the appearance of Viols,
madrigals were more often played than sung.

But let me hasten to tell you it was not

for the playing of madrigals alone that Viol
parties were organised. Certainly not! It
was for the earnest performance of those
complicated pieces called "Fantasies." These
were written for three, four, and six Viols,
and were alone esteemed as "solid and good
musik." They were "solemnly composed
with much art and invention," and for their
perfect performance chests of six Viols were
generally to be found in the houses of most
enthusiastic amateurs.

A description of one of these chests of
Viols is given by Purcell's friend, Dr
Tudway, in a letter to his son at Cambridge:

"A chest of viols was a large hutch with
several apartments and partitions in it, each
partition was lined with green baize to keep
the instruments from being injured by the
weather. Every instrument was sized in
bigness according to the part played on it:
the least size played the treble part, the
tenor and all other parts were played by a
larger sized viol; the bass by the largest
size. They had six strings each, and the
necks of the instruments were fretted. (The
highest) note I believe upon the treble viol
was not higher than G or A."

This treble Viol which Dr Tudway
mentions is thought to have been a very
fashionable instrument at one time. Such
numbers were sent out of the workshops of
Guerson and other Parisian makers that
there is little doubt that the eighteenth-
century ladies of quality followed in the foot-
steps of their sisters of the vielle, and took
the Treble Viol (metaphorically) to their
hearts. But it was not the treble viol alone
that they welcomed thus; they likewise
favoured the Viola da Gamba, or bass viol,
and not only played on it, but made it the
custom to hang it on the wall and use it
when there was any lull in the conversation.

Ben Jonson alludes to this practice and
mentions it as an aid to love-making:

"In making love to her never fear to be
out, for you may have a pipe of tobacco, or
a bass viol which shall hang o' the wall."

In William Gifford's notes to Ben Jonson's
works, he says:

"It appears from numerous passages in
our old plays, that a Viola da Gamba, or bass
viol as Jonson calls it in subsequent passages,

was an indispensable piece of furniture in every fashionable house, where it hung up in the best chamber much as the guitar does in Spain and the violin in Italy, to be played on at will, and to fill up the void of conversation. And it is well known that Sir Andrew Aguecheek could play upon it as he spoke the languages, word for word without book !"

Solo players of the different viols do not appear to have been over numerous. The praises of one of the earliest is sung by Boccaccio, who says Minico d'Arezzio was a great player on the viol, and much in favour with Peter of Roan, King of Sicily. This statement gives point to the supposition that the viol was first in use in Italy. It was only employed for good music as Dr Burney says: "If music for dancing was required, a servant was called in to play the bagpipe."

In England John Jenkins, born at Maidstone in Kent, seems to have taken precedent as a viol player. This talented little man, now chiefly remembered as the author of the famous round "A boat, a boat," was evidently a small but enthusiastic person, for one of his eulogisers describes him as:

"Though a little man, yet he had a great soul." A Norfolk family of the name of Deerham, took great interest in him, and aided him in his studies till he became one of Charles I.'s Court musicians. That monarch appears to have marvelled much at little Johnnie's wonderful performances on the different viols, but more especially on the difficult lyra-viol on which Jenkins excelled.

Theodore Stefkins and his two sons are also quoted as fine performers during the latter part of the fifteenth century.

In France, two players named Mangard and Hotman became very celebrated, and though their popularity was equal, yet they were admired for different qualities : Mangard for brilliancy of execution, and Hotman for the beautiful singing tone he produced. He was also a composer of talent, and is quoted as the first man to write short legato pieces for the Viol.

In the Royal bands (so called) Violins had been included since the time of Queen Elizabeth, who, like most of Henry VIII.'s children, was a skilled musician, and, whom Debourg maintains, was a violinist as well as a virginal player. Year by year the number of stringed instruments in the bands

increased, and judging by the growing pay-
ments made to the instrumentalists, both
player and instrument slowly grew in esteem.

The annual amount paid to the fiddlers
in Queen Elizabeth's time was £230, 6s. 8d.,
and a year later in the Royal book of
expenditure is found the following entry:

"Item: to the vyolons; being viz. of
them 20d. per diam for their wages, and
£16, 2s. 6d. for their liveries, in all per
annum £325, 15s."

Charles I.'s band numbered eleven
"vyolons," amongst fifty-eight musicians;
but it was not until the Restoration of
Charles II. that the Royal band was entirely
composed of stringed instruments. This gay
monarch returning fresh from the French
Court and its music, established in imitation
of Louis XIV. the celebrated band called
the "Four and Twenty Fiddlers." It was
composed of six violins, six counter tenors,
six tenors and six basses, and the honour
of conducting it fell to the hands of
such talented musicians as Baltzar, who
astounded fiddlers by his invention of the
shift, Henry Purcell, poor John Bannister,
who was dismissed for remarking that

"English fiddles surpassed French ones,"
and Pelham Humphreys who hustled and
bustled the king's musicians into playing
French music and enlivening the Court with
Lulli's graceful airs and gavottes. The gay
monarch appeared particularly charmed with
Master Humphrey's innovation and was
seen to nod the Royal head and beat the
Royal foot in appreciation.

So greatly did this prince favour his band
that he would have them play before him
on every possible occasion, even in church.
This last practice of the king's greatly
irritated John Evelyn, who, in his description
of a visit to the Royal Chapel, says:

"Instead of an organ a concert of the king's
four and twenty violins was introduced,
better suiting a tavern than a church."

Pepys, who himself played on several
instruments, and often "rose by candle-light
and spent the morning in fiddling till time to
go to the office," heard the "Four and Twenty
Fiddlers" on more fitting occasions. Once at
Whitehall, where he considered that they had
been "brought by practice to play very just."
Another time on Coronation Day, 23rd April,
1661, he describes taking a great deal of

pleasure "to go up and down and look upon the ladies and to hear the music of all sorts; and above all the twenty-four violins."

In France a Royal band had existed since the time of Louis XIII. under the title of the "Twenty-Four Violins of the King's Chamber." These violinists were elevated from the position of mere minstrels and given the title of "Musiciens en Charge," with a prospect of being admitted to the "Chappell du Roi." Their duties consisted in playing for all the Court balls, performing airs, minuets, correntes, rigaudents, etc., in the king's antechamber, during his dinner, on his birthday, on any fête-day or great occasion.

The passionate love of what were termed *Ballets de Cour*, a combination of dancing and the play, often caused the versatile violinists to turn their attention to this form of amusement for the diversion of their Royal Master, Louis XIV. One most amusing ballet called the *Ballet des doubles Femmes* was a great favourite, and frequently and enthusiastically encored.

In this they dressed up as old women, and put masks on the back of their heads; they then walked in backwards, giving the ludicrous

effect of playing behind their backs.　A most
flattering account of their performance is
given by Pere Mersennus.

He says :

"Whoever hears the twenty-four fidicenists
of the king with six barbitons (basses) to each
part namely : bass-tenor counter-tenor, and
treble must readily confess that there can
be nothing sweeter or pleasanter."

Many promising violinists made their
début in Louis XIV. and Charles II.'s bands.
I say *violinists* with confidence, for Cinderella,
like the Violin, had commenced to make its
appearance from the Brescian workshops
when Viols were still in their zenith.　Humbly
it took its place amongst the Viol family,
receiving small consideration and scanty
admiration.　Harsh in tone it was considered
to destroy the delicate balance of the con-
certed viols, and to cover the piercing tone
of the intruder, a greater number of Bass
Viols were always added.

Those who have heard the gentle tones of
the Viol, will not wonder that ears accustomed
to such a soothing sound could not appreciate
the high pitch and roughness of the imperfect
Violin.　Thomas Mace, the Violist, and John

Playford, a music publisher of the period, give an amusing idea of the low esteem in which the Violin was held. Mace's instructions to make a "true and sizeable Chest of Viols" has a smack of the cookery book.

He says:

"After all this ou may add to your presse a pair of violins to be in readiness for any extraordinarily jolly or jocund consort occasion; but *never use them* but with the provisio, viz.: Be sure you make an equal provision for them by addition and strength of basses so that they may not outcry the rest of the music (the basses especially)."

John Playford says:

"The treble violin is a cheerful and sprightly instrument," and he instructs the pupil to hold it thus:

"First the violin is usually played above hand, the neck thereof being held by the left hand, the lower part must be rested on the left breast a little below the shoulder."

These primitive instructions and remarks about the Violin and its method have quite a pathetic ring about them. They are so evidently written by men who secretly frown on the little impostor, and look upon it as a white elephant. Considered unworthy of a separate instruction book, professors of the Viol were content to include a few observations about it, at the end of their *Viol Tutors*; and in so doing, showed that the true root of their scanty remarks was a lack of knowledge. So absorbed were professors and pupils in the dear old Viols that they had no time to spare for the study of the more difficult violin, and thus the king of stringed instruments was compelled to patiently await the coming of a master hand to place it on its rightful throne.

Description of the various Viols.

According to Fetis, Viols were first made in Nuremburg at the beginning of the fifteenth century, and later in Italy.

The Italian model first appeared from the hands of Joan Kerlino of Brescia, 1449, and was universally adopted.

Viols were divided into two classes:

Viola da Braccio: which were rested against the breast or on the knee.

Viola da Gamba: bass instruments which were held between the knees like a 'cello.

The *Viola da Braccio* were of three kinds:

treble, tenor, and alto ; these, with the Viola da Gamba, corresponded to our modern quartette of instruments, with the exception of the tenor Viol, which is now superseded by the second Violin. Besides the above-mentioned quartette, there was the Violone, the largest of all the Viols. This has retained its original form, and is now our familiar double bass of present day orchestras.

Viols were strung with four, five and six strings. Those with four were tuned in fourths ; and those with five and six also in fourths, but with a major third intervening. The six-stringed Viol survived the longest, lasting about one hundred and fifty years.

Beside the above-mentioned fundamental instruments, there were others which were derived from them :

Viola Bastarda : a development of the Viola da Gamba. This was slightly longer, had six or seven strings, and was much in favour for accompanying the voice.

At one time sympathetic wire strings were added to it ; these passed through holes in the bridge and under the finger-board to the peg-box ; they were tuned chromatically and diatonically.

Viola d'Amore: a development of the treble member of the Viola da Braccio class. This was and is a most beautiful instrument. It had six or seven gut strings and sensitive wire strings beneath.

In Germany this instrument was much favoured, its exquisite arpeggios making an effective accompaniment to the singing voice. At the present day it courts both admirers and executants. Meyerbeer uses it as an accompaniment to the romance sung in the first act of the *Huguenots.*

Viola Pomposa: invented by Sebastian Bach about 1720. This resembled a small violoncello. The tuning was the same as our modern 'cello, with the addition of an upper sixth. Mastin Hoffmann, a Leipzig fiddle-maker, constructed this instrument under Bach's directions.

Viola di Bordone or Barytone: resembled the Viola da Gamba in shape and size. It had six and seven strings, and a double finger-board and bridge. The gut strings passed over one bridge and finger-board, and the wire strings passed over the second. This instrument was greatly in favour in Germany during the latter part of the sixteenth century. Joseph Hayden com-

posed sixty-three pieces expressly for the
Viola di Bordone. The South Kensington
Museum owns a fine specimen ; the scroll
bears an exquisitely carved figure of Apollo,
and the instrument is most handsomely
inlaid.

Besides the Viola da Braccio and Viola
da Gamba class, Italy owned the Lyra
Viols, which were also treble and bass.
They sported an immense number of strings,
varying from twelve to twenty or more, and
were very difficult, owing to the necessarily
wide finger-board. They were chiefly played
in churches.

The earliest viols retained the mediæval
guitar-shaped peg box ; as they grew in
favour, this gave place to the modern
system. At first the improved peg-box
was surmounted by a carved human animal
or grotesque head. Many celebrated artists
exercised their talents in fashioning these,
and produced beautiful little gems. The
custom did not long remain in favour as
Viol makers could not afford the expense
of employing individual artists to complete
their work, and therefore substituted the
familiar fiddle scroll which they could
carve themselves.

The finger-boards of the primitive Viols were marked off in chromatic intervals, which extended about two octaves.

The tuning of the Viols was based on the contemporary vocal music. The methods of notation were two, termed "Lyra way (by letters) and Gamut way (by notes)."

Jean Ott and Hans Frey of Nuremburg are the supposed first makers in Germany, and Joan Kerlino, 1449, the first Italian maker. Gasparo da Salo, Maggini, and all the celebrated fiddle-makers up to the middle of the eighteenth century, manufactured viols. In England Thomas Mace in "Musicks Monument," (1676,) quotes Aldred Jay and Bolles and Rosse, as being "the highest in esteem":

". . . . One bass of Bolles I have known valued at £100. These were old; but we have now very excellent good workmen who no doubt can work as well as these, if they be as well paid for their work as they were; yet we chiefly value old instruments before new; for by experience they are found to be far the best."

ITALIAN MAKERS

CHAT III.

ITALIAN MAKERS—VIOLINS FROM GASPARO DA SALO TO ANTONIUS STRADIVARIUS.

IN 1602 there lived and worked in the little town of Brescia in Lombardy, two men whose names were destined to become as familiar to lovers of the violin as Chaucer and Gower are to lovers of poetry: I mean Gasparo da Salo and his young pupil Gio Paolo Maggini.

Quite unconscious of the "monumental pomp of age" which their handicraft was destined to support, these two men in their workshop under the blue Italian sky, dexterously carved, glued, and stained the violins which after three hundred years still sing their master's names. Simply and earnestly they did their work, and knowingly or unknowingly, put a something into each individual curve, bend, or round, which would ever recall the "touch of the vanished hand."

How interesting it is to observe an expert spelling out the name of an old fiddle by the aid of this "touch of the vanished hand." How eagerly he seeks it and finds it with the help of that alphabet which lies concealed in the colour, shape, height and curves of an old violin.

Long before it was definitely known that Maggini was old da Salo's pupil, experts had ascertained the fact by finding the influence of da Salo's work in the young Maggini's productions, and, more wonderful than this, they had discovered that some of da Salo's violins, though labelled with his name, were really Maggini's work, simply through the incontestable evidence of the "touch of the vanished hand."

Of old Gasparo da Salo little is known. Time, the effacer, has smoothed away all knowledge of the real man, and, as neither Gasparo or Maggini dated their violins, it is only surmised that he was born at a little town called Salo on the borders of Lake Garda, Lombardy, about 1510, and that he died at a ripe old age about 1609.

Whether he was industrious or idle, generous or ungenerous, happy or unhappy, loved or unloved, wise, stupid, married, single,

an admirer of Titian's art, or a condemner
of Galileo's theories (great questions in those
days) is not known.   Old Father Time
grumpily says: "I can remember no more,
only that da Salo lived, manufactured violins,
instructed the young Maggini in the art of
violin-making and—died."

Undoubtedly the finest work of this maker
was put into his tenors and basses, the
violins are generally voted rather rough,
though opinions differ vastly on the subject.
One eminent French writer speaks of da
Salo's *ff*'s as "disgraceful," and his "varnish
almost black"; another writer that the
varnish was excellent and of a deep brown;
another, that his work was highly finished
and the model long and high, which is
again contradicted by a fourth writer, who
says that his models varied in height and
his work was rough.   The explanation of
this diversity of opinion is evident: da Salo's
work was unequal because he was feeling
his way, and only now and again succeeded
in producing a fine instrument.

Mr Haweis in *Old Violins* speaks of a
fine specimen of da Salo which was the
property of Lord Amherst.   He mentions
playing on it, and says the A and D strings

were rich and pure, the 1st and 4th rather
muffled, but on the whole, "the tone is
mellow and powerful."

Another fine instrument of this maker is
the one called the "Treasury Violin," which
I here quote, although opinions differ as
to its authenticity. This violin was at one
time the property of the Swedish violinist,
Ole Bull, and was exhibited by him in London
in 1862 at a conversazione held by the
Musical Society in St James' Hall. The
following description was attached to it:—

"The celebrated 'Treasury Violin' of
Innspruck by Gaspar di Salo with Caryatides
by Benvenuto Cellini, sculptured by command
of Cardinal Aldobrandini, and by him presented to the Museum of Innspruck in the
Tyrol. After the assault upon the said city
by the French in 1809, the Museum was
plundered and the violin carried to Vienna,
where the Councillor Rhehazek placed this
unique gem in his celebrated collection of
ancient musical instruments, refusing to sell
it at any price. He left it by will to Ole
Bull in 1842 ; up to that period it had never
been played upon."

Ole Bull for many years used a Guarnerius

and an Amati, but both these instruments
were discarded when he became possessed
of his cherished Gasparo da Salo. Here is
the great *virtuoso's* story of it in his own
words:

"Well, in 1839 I gave sixteen concerts at
Vienna and then Rhehazek was the great
violin collector. I saw at his house this
violin for the first time. I just went wild
over it. 'Will you sell it?' I asked. 'Yes,'
was the reply, 'for one quarter of all Vienna.'
Now Rhehazek was really as poor as a church
mouse. Though he had no end of money
put out in the most valuable instruments,
he never sold any of them unless when
forced by hunger. I invited Rhehazek to
my concerts. I wanted to buy the violin
so much that I made him some tempting
offers. One day he said to me, 'See here,
Ole Bull, if I do sell the violin, you shall
have the preference at four thousand ducats.'
'Agreed,' I cried, though I knew it was a big
sum.

"That violin came strolling, or playing
rather, through my brain for some years.
It was in 1841, I was in Leipsic giving
concerts. Liszt was there, and so also was

Mendelssohn. One day we were all dining together. We were having a splendid time. During the dinner came an immense letter with a seal—an official document. Said Mendelssohn, 'Use no ceremony; open your letter.' 'What an awful seal!' cried Liszt. 'With your permission,' said I, and I opened the letter. It was from Rhehazek's son, for the collector was dead. His father had said that the violin should be offered to me at the price he had mentioned. I told Liszt and Mendelssohn about the price. 'You man from Norway, you are crazy,' said Liszt. 'Unheard of extravagance, which only a fiddler is capable of,' exclaimed Mendelssohn. 'Have you ever played on it? Have you ever tried it?' they both enquired. 'Never,' I answered, 'for it cannot be played on at all just now.'

"I never was happier than when I felt sure that the prize was mine. Originally the bridge was of boxwood, with two fishes carved on it—that was the zodiacal sign of my birthday, February—which was a good sign. Oh, the good times that violin and I have had! As to its history, Rhehazek told me that in 1809, when Innspruck was taken by the French, the

soldiers sacked the town. This violin had
been placed in the Innspruck Museum by
Cardinal Aldobrandini at the close of the
sixteenth century. A French soldier looted
it, and sold it to Rhehazek, for a trifle. This
is the same violin that I played on when
I first came to the United States, in the
Park Theatre. That was on Evacuation
Day, 1843. I went to the Astor House,
and made a joke—I am quite capable of
doing such things. It was the day when
John Bull went out and Ole Bull came in.
I remember that at the very first concert
one of my strings broke, and I had to work
out my piece on the three strings, and it
was supposed I did it on purpose."

Da Salo's fiddles are scarce and fetch a
good price, but the *virtuoso* does not seek
them ; the collector alone buys them (when
he can) as interesting specimens of the work
of the man, who by some is considered the
inventor of the violin, and, even if not the
inventor, still was certainly one of the first
to manufacture them, and spread those seeds
of progress which were gathered by his
pupil, Maggini, and ripened by Maggini's
successors.

Gio: Paolo Maggini.

Gio: Paolo Maggini, da Salo's pupil, was
born in Brescia in 1581.   His parents, it is
thought, were simple country folk, who settled
in Brescia before the birth of the little Paolo
who arrived to cheer his father's advanced
years.

At what age he was apprenticed to old
Gasparo da Salo is not certain, it is only
definitely known that when he was twenty-
one (in 1602) he was working under that
veteran maker's guidance, and probably
turning out copies of his master's models.
Arrived at the age of thirty-four (nearly
the time specified by Byron as the "yellow-
leaf") he married Anna Forestio, a lady
who among other virtues was blessed with
a dowry, and probably such a wifely faith
in her husband's talents that Maggini, the
married man, set up a business of his own,
and started chiselling fiddles in earnest.

Being a man of genius, he was not long
in deserting the paths of da Salo and his
forerunners, and turning his attention to
those innovations which have remained
component parts of every violin.   His first

breaking away from tradition was in
altering the old manner of cutting the
wood. Heretofore it had always been the
custom to cut the wood for Viols in what
is termed "slab fashion." Da Salo followed
the ancient custom, and made his violins
in this way, but Maggini with Herculean
strength, threw aside tradition and custom
and cut the wood wedge-ways; just as one
cuts a slice out of a melon. Soon he
attained more finish in his work, made his
models larger than da Salo's, his $f\!f$'s much
smoother, and introduced corner blocks
and linings such as are now used. His
varnish was of an excellent quality, with
pure orange and yellow tints, and also a
touch of brown in some of his earlier
instruments. Most of his fiddles are double
purfled, which gives them a certain dis-
tinctiveness, and makes them look larger
than they really are. As to the tone, it is
powerful, but has neither the purity of an
Amati nor the brilliancy of a Stradivarius,
and the muffled quality is somewhat
suggestive of a Viol.

No certificate of Maggini's death is as
yet forthcoming, so it is conjectured that
he died of the cruel plague which

ravaged Brescia in 1623, and, being carried
to one of the plague-houses, was hastily
buried. He was only fifty-one, and the
result of his life's work counted but fifty
fiddles and under two dozen tenors and
violoncellos. Truly a small number, but
as Maggini is considered to have had independent means, he was thus able to do
his work more for art's sake, and leave
those "footprints on the sands of time"
which have helped his successors and even
inspired Stradivarius to make his "Long
pattern Strads." Some of Maggini's finest
fiddles have been in the hands of many
a great *virtuoso* ; Ole Bull, Leonard, Vieux-
temps, all possessed Maggini's, and that
elegant Belgian artist, de Beriot, had two
fine specimens, one of which he picked up
in an old curiosity shop in Paris, for fifteen
francs. This instrument now belongs to
the Prince de Chimey, and is considered
of high value.

.   .   .   .

While da Salo and Maggini in Brescia
were gradually solving the problem of
acquiring greater power of tone, Andrea
Amati and his two sons, Antonio and
Hieronymus, were turning their attention

to purity and sweetness in Cremona. What da Salo and Maggini had gained in power, the Amatis gained in sweetness, and in so doing forged the great link between the old Brescian makers and Stradivarius, who so grandly combined the three qualities—sweetness, purity, and power.

Rome was not built in a day, nor was this perfection hastily accomplished, for that which da Salo, Maggini and the Amatis commenced was left for another generation to perfect after a lapse of nearly a hundred years.

Of old Andrea Amati, the founder of the Cremona violin family, very little is definitely known. He was born about 1520, is quoted as one of a noble family who intermarried with people of rank, and seems to have been orignally a maker of rebecs, Viola da Gamba, and Viola da Braccio. Where he acquired his knowledge of Violin-making is undiscovered, and it is only conjectured from the resemblance of his *ff*'s. to these of Gasparo da Salo, that he may have visited Brescia and, seeing da Salo's work, became fired with the ambition to contrive something of the same kind.

Few of Andrea Amati's Violins are now

extant, and the existing ones are in poor preservation, but from these it is judged that he used excellent wood, good amber-coloured varnish, made his models smaller than Maggini or da Salo, and that his style and work was altogether an advancement on the Brescian makers. He died about 1577, leaving his two sons, Antonio and Hieronymus (born about 1550), to carry on the business after his death.

These two brothers worked conjointly for many years, and labelled the violins, which were their united efforts, with both their names. Their work was most excellent, and though they kept to their father's model, they made slight improvements which were advantageous. But with all their cleverness they did not succeed in adding one atom of power to the already sweet Amati tone. Delicacy, charm, purity, all these qualities are found in the early Amati fiddles, but the growth of power still remained the chief victory of the Brescian makers.

Fortunately for the forthcoming generations of fiddle-makers, worthy Hieronymus, the cleverer of the two brothers, was not too engrossed in the exquisite pleasure of fiddle-making to omit seeing the charms of a lady named Madalina Lattazini, whom he wooed and married.

After this event Hieronymus proceeded to dissolve partnership with his brother Antonio, and at the same time to adopt a model of his own. These individual efforts of Hieronymus, however, were not very successful, and it remained for his little son, Nicolo, born 13th September 1596, to add genius to his father's talents, and raise the art of violin-making to great heights.

An assiduous worker, Nicolo, in his youth learnt the art of violin-making in his father's shop, and contented himself with copying the Antonio and Hieronymus model. From the very first his genius is said to have been discernible, and, though in his early attempts he kept to the traditions of the Amati family, he rapidly mastered and outstrode them. The Amati model was always delicate and graceful, but Nicolo's calculations as to proportions made his instruments surpass those of his predecessors in that respect. His model, as a rule, was a small one, but his finest instruments were larger than any made by the Amati family. These are generally known as the "Grand Amati," and it was this

E

pattern that his pupil Stradivarius afterwards laboured so assiduously to bring to
perfection.

Nicolo Amati's small-pattern violins can
be purchased from about £80 to £100, but
his Grand Amati pattern are worth about
£200. A Nicolo Amati, which was the
property of Mr Betts, was valued at £250,
and one which belonged to Sir William
Curtis, was put up for auction at 150 guineas,
and bought for 185. This violin was dated
1647, and was described in the catalogue
as "one of the most beautiful and finest in
the whole world."

During his lifetime Nicolo's instruments
were highly esteemed, and many were the
orders he received from the nobles of Verona,
Florence, Tuscany, and also from countries
beyond Italy.

His imitators were numerous, and his
pupils many and distinguished, numbering
among them such names as Grancino,
Ruggieri, Albani, Cappa, Andrea Guarnerius
and Antonius Stradivarius.

Andrea Guarnerius, uncle of the great
Joseph Guarnerius del Gesu, transmitted
through his son the skill he learnt in Nicolo's
shop; and Antonius Stradivarius, the as-

siduous and gifted student, afterwards
carried his master's work to that exquisite
perfection which has placed his own instruments in unassailable pre-eminence.

Nicolo Amati died 12th August 1684,
leaving one son, Geronimico, who was also
a fiddle-maker, but of far less importance
than his father—in fact Nicolo was the last
and the greatest of all the Amati family.
His calculations as to thickness of wood,
elevation of belly and back, far surpassed
those of his predecessors, and added to his
instruments a slight touch of power which
the former members of his family had failed
to attain.

ANTONIUS STRADIVARIUS. *Born* 1644, *died*
   *1737. Son of Signor Alessandro Stradi-
   varius and Signora Anna Moroni.*

There is no name in the history of violin-
making about which there clings so much
interest as that of Antonius Stradivarius.
Yet, should you visit Cremona to-day,
ardently wishing to discover something more
of him, you will find that this prophet of
glue-pots and wizard of curves has inherited
a prophet's fate, "having no honour in his

own country." If your zeal leads you to rashly ask questions, your reward will be astonishment on the part of the Cremonese, who seem quite unaware that their town was once famous for its violins. To them the name of Stradivarius suggests some doctor, priest, or barrister; but of Antonius Stradivarius, the fiddle-maker, they know little or nothing.

It is satisfactory to feel that during his lifetime this great artist did not suffer from any neglect from his fellow-citizens, for they loved "The plain white-aproned man who stood at work patient and accurate, full fourscore years." They revered his patience and temperance, and admired the frugality which brought him fame and money.

Being thorough, economical, highly-gifted and industrious, Strad's success in life was an assured fact. But, how he worked! Even in the last years of his life, when his hand had somewhat lost its cunning, he never ceased; in fact, the hale and hearty old man of ninety was so proud of his capabilities that he often affixed his age to the labels of his later instruments.

A great French writer has epitomised Strad's life as "work and children," a remark which has often caused me to ruminate as to whether Stradivarius would have been quite so industrious, minus the two Signora Stradivaris and the eleven olive branches. After consideration I have come to the conclusion that, in all probability, he might have remained a second-rate fiddle-maker all his life, but for that family which simply *had* to be supported. Truly, the fiddle-making world owes a deep debt of gratitude *à ces dames* and the eleven children!

Strad's primary work commenced when about fourteen, in Nicolo Amati's shop. Here, side by side, with the more sober Andrea Guarnerius, he was initiated in all the exquisite artifices of the violin craft. Here, under his master's scrutiny, he daily scraped and carved his way to greater perfection. Here, reposing from his labours, he laughed with the gay little rogue, Joseph Guarnerius (son of Andrea), or chatted with Grancino and Ruggieri. Here his dexterous hands are said to have made many a violin which was labelled Nicolas Amati, and here he dreamed love dreams of Francesca Ferabosca, a widow ten years his senior, whom he eventually married when he was but eighteen years old.

The union was solemnised at the Church of St Agatha, and the Marriage Register of the parish recounts:

"On the 4th July 1667, having three times published the banns on feast days, the first on 26th June, which was a Sunday, the second on the 29th, the feast day of St Peter, the third on Sunday the 3rd July, announcing the marriage which Signor Antonio Stradivari of the parish of St Cecilia, intended to contract with Signora Francesca Ferabosca of my parish; I hereby declare that no impediment having arisen, I, the Reverend Pietro Guallo, Parish Priest of the Collegiate and renowned Church of St Agata in Cremona, have united them to-day, here, in my Church, in the holy bond of matrimony, in the presence of the two hereafter mentioned witnesses, namely Signor Francesco Ferabosco, of the Parish of St Agata, and of Signor ———" (this remains unfilled).

After this marriage came the more earnest work and vigorous *aplomb* of the man who sees the possibilities of the game of life spreading out before him; and in 1679 an opportunity for a display of this energy was

opened to him. This *bonne chance* came
through the retirement from business of his
veteran master, Nicolo Amati, then the
acknowledged head of violin-making. Cute
Stradivarius, seeing his chance, seized, so to
speak, the prophet's mantle and wrapped it
firmly about him.

Far too astute to fly in the face of Amati's
theories, Stradivarius at this period, contented
himself by taking his master's larger pattern
as his model. Mr Hart says:

"The arching is identical, the corners are
treated similarly, the sound-hole is quite
Amati-like in form, yet easily distinguished
by its extreme delicacy. The scroll is a
thorough imitation of Amati, and presents a
singular contrast to the vigorous individuality
which Stradivarius displayed in this portion
of his work a few years later."

He also remarks that:

"In these earlier specimens there is a
singular absence of handsome wood."

Strad's thrifty habits probably caused him
to make a success of his first year's venture
in business, for in 1680, when he was thirty-
six, he moved his premises into the very

heart of Cremona's fiddle-making world:
No. 1 Piazza St Domenico (now Piazza Roma).
Here, with a white woollen cap on his head
in the winter, a white cotton cap in the
summer, and a white leather apron to protect
his clothes from chips and glue, tall, thin
Stradivarius laboured incessantly to the end
of his days.   He bought this house, known
as No. 1 Piazza Roma, from a Cremonese
family for about £280.   It was a narrow
building, consisting of three floors and large
underground cellars.   On the ground-floor
was the shop, the parlour, the kitchen, and
at the other end of the courtyard, the store-
room.   On the next floor, another four rooms,
three on the next, and then came the attic
above, a sort of covered terrace which was
called " Seccadour," or " drying-place "; here
it was customary for the Cremonese to dry
their linen and fruit.

    In this quiet retreat Strad worked during
the summer months; suspended between
earth and sky, he "ascended to the highest
heaven of invention."   Here, in the silence
which was only occasionally disturbed by
the faint sounds from the town beneath,
he followed the dictates of his own fancy,
pondering the great problems of thickness,

height, length, breadth, etc., and wielding
the witchery of glue-pot and sand-paper at
will. Here he attained that maturity of
experience which gave him power to produce
instruments free from his master's influence:
a flatter form, a gracefully reclining sound-
hole, and a beautiful individuality in the
shape of the scroll. And here he carefully
copied out on the fly-leaf of his Bible the
recipe for his wonderful varnish; the secret
of which has been so jealously guarded by
his descendants, that the present generation
count it a lost art.

On 20th May 1698, his first wife, Francesca
Ferabosca, then about fifty-eight, died, and
her husband, ten years her junior, buried her
in a conspicuously sumptuous manner for
those days. Among the items of her funeral
expenses, which exceeded £20, are fees paid
to fourteen priests and choir-boys, to over a
hundred fathers of different denominations,
to twelve torch-bearers; for the "Velvet and
gold pall of the Cathedral," for "grave-diggers
with capes," for the "Big Bell," the bells of
St Matteo and Domenico, and the little bells
of the Cathedral, etc. From all of which
careful Strad, considering himself overcharged,
deducts eight lires.

The account of her death and burial reads
as follows, in the Parish Register of St
Matteo:

"Francesca Ferabosca, wife of Signor
Antonius Stradivari, recommended to God,
and fortified by the Sacraments of Penance,
Holy Eucharist, and Extreme Unction, died
at the age of about sixty years. Her body
was carried into the Church of St Domenico."

The year following, Stradivarius again
entered into the bonds of matrimony, marry-
ing on this occasion Signora Antonia
Zambelli, in the parish of St Donato, on the
24th August 1699.

By this time his reputation as a violin
maker was well established, and the former
customers of Nicolo Amati, recognising his
genius, readily accepted him in the place of
his master. In 1684, he had numbered
amongst his noble patrons James II. of
England, the Duke of Florence, and other
notabilities, for whom he made instruments
alla posta (expressly). For these *alla
posta* orders, he executed very special
designs, not only for the fiddles and their
ornamentation, but also for the minutest
details of their cases. This thoroughness

of Strad's often caused great delays in the
delivery of the instruments, which, however,
could not be hastened by any pressure from
his distinguished patrons.

On one occasion, when making a set of
instruments for the Spanish Court, Strad
was so dilatory that the director of the
king's music was sent to Cremona with
strict orders to remain there until they
were completed. He stayed three weeks,
but returned in triumph with the delayed
"concerto" On another occasion Strad
writes to a "most esteemed and illustrious
sir," saying he has been unable to send the
violin "in consequence of having to wait
continually for some one to convey it to
you," and only through the departure of
"the bare-footed father, San Mauro" is he
enabled to deliver his order: "He has
promised to let you have it immediately, I
therefore beg that you will forgive me for
not having sent it earlier, and I hope you
will be pleased with it." He ends his
letter by "kissing your hands and making
obeisance" and remaining "your Excellency's
most humble and devoted servant, Antonius
Stradivari."

In 1687, he executed a fine concerto of

instruments for the King of Spain, these were beautifully ornamented, having a purfling of ivory. One of the Violins of this quintette once belonged to Ole Bull, through whose hands a number of notable fiddles passed at one time and another.

Three years later, in 1690, the Marquis Bartholomeo Arbato writes to Strad acknowledging the famous " concerto " of instruments made for the Grand Duke of Tuscany :

" I assure you the prince has accepted your instruments with more pleasure than I could expect. The players in the orchestra are unanimous in expressing appreciation. They declare your instruments to be quite perfect ; they all say they never heard a violoncello with such a tone as yours. My having brought to the knowledge of such a person as His Highness your great skill, will doubtless procure you many orders from his exalted house."

Before 1792, one of these *chefs d œuvres* of Strad's had disappeared from the ducal collection, when, where, or how is an unsolved mystery. Three years later the missing instrument turned up in the hands of a certain Giovanni Felice Mosell, a Florentine

musician and composer, who sold it to
Mr David Ker of Portavoe, Ireland, for about
£24. Mr Ker, who was a great book
collector, appears to have had no particular
interest in violins, and only bought this one
at the instigation of Angelica Kauffmann, to
whom he was at the time sitting for his
portrait. Emersed in his book collecting,
he returned with the exquisite "Tuscan
Strad" to Ireland, where it was put away
at one of his houses called "Glory Holes."
For about fifty years it remained *perdu*, and,
only on the death of Mr Ker, was discovered
by his executors and sold by his son to Mr
F. Ricardo for £240. In 1888, its present
owners, Messrs W. E. Hill & Sons, having
watched the whereabouts of this magnificent
instrument for several years, bought it for a
sum running into four figures.

The chief characteristic of the "Tuscan
Strad" is its marvellous preservation — no
cracks, no repairs and no signs of wear
except where the chin rests. Here and on
the back the varnish is slightly rubbed off.
The delicate scroll still preserves the painted
outline with which it was Strad's custom to
pick out his work. In nearly every other
specimen except the "Messie," this running

is either slightly or entirely rubbed off. The varnish is of a clear, reddish brown, with an undercurrent of orange. The tone is ringing as a bell, and the corners as sharp and unspoiled as if just cut by Stradivarius' hand. Altogether a unique instrument this, and one cannot wonder that Herr Joachim, who is such a great lover of the Strad fiddle, wrote to its present owners, when he heard of it, and begged that it might be kept for him to see.

From this time till his death (1737), Stradivarius made his finest instruments, amongst them the notable "Pucelle" (labelled 1709). This was one of Tarisios' discoveries, and reached Paris about 1840. The interior of this fiddle was found by Monsieur Vuillaume to be entirely untouched, the bass bar remaining just as Stradivarius had fixed it. The varnish is a great contrast to the "Tuscan," being of a soft yellowy brown. It was first owned by Monsieur le Roy, a French banker, and on his death, passed into the possession of his heir, Monsieur Glaudey, in whose family it still remains. It is valued at over £900.

In the same year he made the beautiful violin which belonged to "Ernst." This was purchased for Lady Hallé for the sum of £500, and presented to her by Earl Dudley and others. In 1711, the "Parke," which has passed through the hands of many enthusiastic collectors. In 1712, Viotti's violin, on which he played till his death; particular interest attaches to this violin, as Viotti was the first *virtuoso* to discover the value and beauty of Strad's violins, from the player's point of view. In 1713, he made Señor Sarasate's beautiful fiddle called the "Boissiér." In 1714, the "Dolphin," on which Strad put the exquisite iridescent varnish from which it takes its name. This fiddle was at one time the treasured possession of Monsieur Alard, Sarasate's master. It is now worth over £1,100.

In 1715, Strad made the fiddle which belonged to Mr Gillot (of pen-making fame), after whom it is named. Of the same year, are the three instruments owned by Professor Joachim, and that superlative fiddle called the "Alard," which, in the opinion of the great experts, Messrs W. E. Hill & Sons, is the "finest of the fine." This fiddle (now the property of Baron Knoop) is one of the most vigorous of Stradivarius' productions. The lower bouts are very broad, the corners

are pulled out as though drawn to the uttermost point between finger and thumb. The
varnish is of a deeper tinge than any of
Strad's other great creations. The tone is
a combination of brilliancy, purity and
tenderness, and the articulation is so free
that the notes flit out as swiftly as a swallow
flies.

In 1716, many more fine instruments
made their *début*, amongst them the
"Cesole" and "Messie" or "Messiah," the
most romantic of all Stradivarius' creations.
This graceful instrument which for years,
was on the verge of appearing to the fiddle-
loving world, emerged after more than a
century of silence, as youthful and fresh-
looking as though just completed in the
Cremona workshop.[1]

The "Cesole" was once the property of
the violinist, Felix Artot, and at his death
passed into the hands of the Count de
Cesole, after whom it is named. The Count
having been a warm friend of Paganini, it
is in the highest degree probable that the
fingers of the great *virtuoso* may have fre-

[1] As the history of the "Messie" also involves an
account of Luigi Tarisio, I have given it a special
place at the end of this chapter.

quently lingered on its ebony fingerboard.
Paganini died at the Count de Cesole's house
at Nice, where the Count surrounded him
with every attention that affection could
suggest.

Some years after Paganini's death, his
friend Berlioz was also at Nice seeking
health, and one night while he lay dreaming
over his dead friend, the sounds of a violin
reached his ear. The music was Paganini's
variations on "The Carnival." Berlioz was
greatly startled, and, rushing to the window,
discovered the player to be Count Cesole.
He was serenading his living friend with
the music of their dead friend, on the glorious
"Cesole Stradivarius."

In 1717, came the "Sasseron," and 1718
the "Maurin." Then, in 1722, the exquisitely
ornamented violin called the "Rode," the
ribs of which are covered with a conventional
design in black. The purfling is inlaid with
ivory and mother-of-pearl. This fiddle,
which was the last of his ornamented ones,
has risen gradually in price from £160, for
which sum it was purchased from Rode by
the Duc d'Olbreuse, to £1,200, which price
was paid for it by Hills in 1890.

The above-mentioned are only a few of

F

this great artist's *chefs d'œuvres*; the colossal labour of cataloguing the two thousand instruments attributed to him is one which has yet to be accomplished, and which, if practicable, would be a most acceptable addition to violin literature.

If an Act of Parliament could be passed in every country, compelling each owner of a Strad to register his precious treasure at a given centre, the number of *known* Strads would be vastly increased. Of course dealers keep a careful account of each Strad that passes through their hands, but there must be numberless others (including those that have been tampered with, for which act there should be a severe punishment) that probably never reach them, and the only remedy is a *census* through compulsory registration.

After 1722, the list of Strad's notable instruments ceases; he was then verging on eighty, and though so vigorous as to be able to continue working, the instruments made in the last fifteen years preceding his death show the shaking hand of the old man.

One fiddle, made six years before his death, belongs to Monsieur Eugène Ysaye, and one he made in 1687, before the appearance of any of his famous instruments, belongs to Herr Jan Kubelik. Those who have heard these two great artists play, will agree, I am sure, that Strad could make a fine fiddle outside that most notable period which commenced in 1690 and ended about 1722.

The great fiddle-maker died in 1737 (but a few months after his second wife), and was buried with her in the vault which he purchased from the Villani family in 1729.

The following is the record of his death, extracted from the Parish Register of St Matteo :

"In the year of our Lord one thousand seven hundred and thirty-seven, on the nineteenth day of the month of December, Signor Antonio Stradivari, a widower aged about ninety-five years, having died yesterday, fortified by the holy Sacraments and comforted by prayers for his soul until the moment he expired. I, Domenico Antonio Stancari, Parish Priest of this Church of St Matteo, have escorted to-day his corpse with funeral pomp to the Church of the very Reverend Fathers of St Domenico in Cremona, where he was buried."

This Church of St Domenico and the

Chapel of the Blessed Virgin of the Rosary,
where Stradivarius was buried, has since been
demolished and the ground turned into a
public garden. The only record that now
remains of his place of interment, is the
following inscription on one of the ornamental
vases in the gardens:

" Here where formerly stood
The CONVENT and CHURCH of
THE DOMENICAN INQUISITORS
The Town Council
Have provided
A pleasant prospect
of trees and flowers
1878."

On the new house which replaces
Stradivarius', the following commemorative
tablet has been placed:

" Here stood the house
in which
ANTONIO STRADIVARI
Brought the violin to its highest perfection
And left to Cremona
An unperishable name as a master of his craft."

These two tablets are the chief public
honours given by his native town to the
gifted man who laboured incessantly for
nearly seventy years in solving those problems

of violin-making which had baffled his predecessors.

The difficulty of his task is only understood when one stops to think of the combined qualities required for the undertaking. He must have had mathematical exactitude, architectural knowledge, knowledge of acoustics, a certain amount of chemical knowledge, and a knowledge of carpentry; also the sure hand of a practised wood-carver, and an artist's eye for form and colour. *Grâce au Dieu* these gifts he intuitively possessed, and their union has given to grateful fiddlers, those perfect instruments which throb and pulsate in response to the artist's touch like a second soul.

Something about the " Messie Strad" and Luigi Tarisio.

Those "Instruments de Luxe," the "Tuscan," " Pucelle," " Rode," " Dolphin," " Alard," etc., are all recognised as grand instruments, exquisitely made and marvellously preserved; each and all claim ardent admiration (and a high price), yet none of them possess the unique interest of the mighty " Messie," or "Messiah," which remained more than a century as silent as any Egyptian sphinx.

One hundred and forty-seven speechless years, after which it emerged delicately beautiful in design, exquisite in workmanship, perfect in varnish, and with such an air of youth that Strad's brush might have touched it but a week before. To look at this fine work of art it is difficult to realise that its almost fairy-like delicacy was conceived by a rugged old man of seventy, who until then had been constructing fiddles of solidity and breadth. Like a mighty giant, weary of playing with mountains, Stradivarius seems to have paused to regain breath by plucking a fragile flower, and weaving it into that lovely thing we call a fiddle.

The label within the "Messie," is dated 1716, twenty years before Stradivarius' death, at which time, it being still among the ninety-one in his possession, it became the property of his son, Paolo, who treasured it carefully until his own death in 1775. Then it was sold to Count Cozio di Salabue, the well-known Italian collector. Here, in the company of the Count's numerous other instruments, it reposed for another fifty years calm and untouched, until the hand of death again intervened in 1824, and caused it to be sold to no less a person than unscrupulous Luigi Tarisio — carpenter, amateur fiddle repairer, and connoisseur.

For the next thirty years the "Messie" was more strictly guarded than ever; no early Victorian mother could have chaperoned her only child more heavily than Luigi chaperoned his treasure. To screen it from the vulgar gaze and ensure its safety, he placed it in an isolated farm named "La Croix," near the village of Fontenato, in Italy, where, in the company of a glorious Guarnerius, it passed its days in the bottom drawer of a rickety old bureau.

Tarisio, in the meantime, successfully continued his cunning game of collecting valuable fiddles from the Italian monks and peasants, on the "exchange no robbery" system, and one fine day, two years later, his shabby figure suddenly appeared in the shop of one of the most fashionable dealers in Paris. At first, the dealer was very much inclined to refuse the seemingly humble pedlar admittance, but Tarisio's calm firmness over-ruled his scruples, and the carpenter was allowed to empty his sack of fiddles on the counter. Out they came from the shabby bag, and

down they went, side by side, in serried ranks :
Amati, Ruggieri, Maggini, etc., all beaming
up into the astonished dealer's face. After
an hour or so Tarisio bid adieu to the much-
impressed dealer ; on the carpenter's shoulder
was an empty sack ; in his pocket a goodly
sum of money. Back he went to Italy again
to add more treasures to his store, and on his
next visit to Paris, he found the doors of all
the French dealers welcomingly opened to
him. This time he made some good bargains,
and the shabby coat and down-at-heel
appearance vanished.

In 1851 he came to England, and his fame
having gone before him, he was received
with open arms as a person of remarkable
capabilities by the English dealers.

It is most regrettable that so little has
been written about this extraordinary man,
who would have sold his very soul to the
devil, if necessary, for the sake of a fiddle.
Signor Patti, Vuillaume, Chanot, and hosts
of others who knew him, were full of anecdotes concerning him, but the only man who
has ever troubled to say something of
Tarisio on paper, was our own Charles Reade
of " Never too Late to Mend " fame.

Mr Reade, who himself was a great fiddle-

collector and connoisseur, knew Tarisio
personally, and in his estimation: "The
man's whole soul was in his fiddles. He
was a great dealer but a greater amateur.
Tarisio had gems by him which no money
would buy from him." To Tarisio, the
acquisition and possession of beautiful fiddles
was far above anything else life could give.
One day when walking with Mr Reade in
Paris, a gorgeous equipage attracted their
attention. Tarisio remarked, "He would
sooner possess *one* Strad than twenty such
carriages."

One of the most amusing anecdotes
Mr Reade gives, is that of Tarisio's hunt for
the Spanish bass. The story runs something like the following:

The great French dealer, George Chanot
(senior) took a trip to Spain in search of
fiddles. He found little of value, and was
about to return to Paris when he saw in
the shop window of a fiddle-maker named
Ortega, in Madrid, the belly of an old bass,
which attracted his quick eye. He examined
it more closely and discovered it to be
unmistakably Stradivarius' work. In walked
Chanot, and in the twinkling of an eye
bought the precious thing for forty francs,

and carried it off in triumph to Paris. A few days later Tarisio comes into Chanot's shop, from Italy. "*Mon dieu*! Chanot, where did you get that Strad belly?"

"*Mon cher*, I picked it up for about forty francs."

"But where—where?" exclaims Tarisio.

"In Spain."

"*Cielo*! from whom?"

"From a dealer named Ortega," and Chanot, seeing Tarisio's ever-increasing excitement, related how he found it and purchased it in Spain.

"I will give you a thousand francs for it," and putting down the sum, Tarisio seized the Strad belly and started there and then for Spain.

No sooner arrived in Madrid, than he sought and found the wretched Ortega who had dared to tamper with Strad's work. From him he ascertained the truth, namely, the bass had been sent to him for repairs by a lady, and as he discovered the belly had many cracks, he had detached it and put on a nice new one. If the Señor wished to view the instrument, he had only to repair to the Señorita's house. She would doubtless allow the "instrument to

show itself." Off rushed Tarisio, all eager-
ness to interview the lady; the instrument
was allowed to "show itself," and the lady
with true Spanish politeness, said, "Sir, 'tis
yours," which in Spain is meaningless.
When Tarisio approached the question of
purchasing it, the Señorita said she could
not part with it; when he named the sum
he would give, she grew sad and said it had
been long in the family; Tarisio added to
his first offer. The lady, seeing he really
wanted to buy, receded still more, until by
continued increasing, he finally offered about
£150, which sum was accepted by the
Señorita.

Tarisio, now the happy possessor of the
complete bass, sailed exultantly for Paris.
In the Channel a storm was raging, the
waves rose high, the ship tossed and pitched
heavily, but never for a moment did the
valiant Tarisio leave hold of his beloved
bass. Clasped tightly in his arms, he
protected it from the mighty tempest, indeed
he would have preferred to die himself
rather than allow anything to happen to
the beloved instrument. When recounting
the horror of the voyage afterwards to
Mr Reade, he said: "Ah, my poor Mr

Reade, the Bass of Spain was all but
lost."

The "Bass of Spain" on its safe arrival
in Paris was given into the hands of
Vuillaume, who (as Mr Reade so delightfully
puts it) "with the help of a sacred vessel
called a glue-pot, soon re-wedded the back and
sides to the belly." Having its members once
again united, the bass was as fine as before
Ortega's meddling, and was sold for £800.

Although Tarisio's dealings with foreign
fiddle-makers necessitated many journeys to
France, England and other countries, his
real home was always in his native Italy.
Shortly before his death he settled in Milan,
where he took an attic at the top of a
second-class restaurant, in the Via Legnano
Porta Tegnaglia. Here he was found one
cold winter's morning in 1854, quite dead.
Round him on every side were priceless
fiddles : nothing else, no luxuries, no comfort,
only fiddles, fiddles, fiddles, and the poor
dead thing whose whole life had been
one long passionate struggle for their
possession.

The moment it was known to Monsieur
Vuillaume that the famous Tarisio was no
more, he journeyed to Italy immediately,

and, being the first dealer in the field, interviewed Tarisio's nephews. From them he purchased the two hundred and forty-six exquisite fiddles, which were crammed into Tarisio's poor little attic, for £3,166. This done, Vuillaume asked Tarisio's sister, "Where is the Messie?" to which she replied that there were still six instruments at the farm called "La Croix," adding that she would conduct him there if he wished.

Arrived at the farm, Monsieur Vuillaume was handed four dusty fiddle cases. Out of the first he took a splendid Strad, the second a beautiful Carlo Bergonzi, and out of the other two, two fine Guadagnini. Then came a pause, and he was directed to open the bottom drawer of a very rickety piece of furniture. To pull this drawer open was no easy task, for two violins were so tightly wedged within that it seemed almost impossible to do so without damaging them. Finally, it was accomplished, and there lay, exposed to view, a grand Joseph Guarnerius del Gesù, and the youthful "Messie," Strad. For a few moments Monsieur Vuillaume gazed at it without a movement; then he tenderly lifted the two beautiful instruments out of their hiding-place and examined them closely :

they were perfect, not a scar or scratch marred their exquisite beauty.

Tarisio's nephews were persuaded to part with the six instruments to Monsieur Vuillaume at a price, and the great dealer returned exultantly to Paris with the beautiful "Messiah."

During the rest of Monsieur Vuillaume's life the "Messie" was placed in a glass case in his shop for inspection, and on his death, became the property of his son-in-law, Delphin Alard. It was then valued at £1,000. Alard left it to his wife in his will, and on her death it was sold to Mr E. Crawford, an enthusiastic amateur, for the largest sum ever paid for a fiddle, £2,000.

The "Messie's" history is romantic, the "Messie's," preservation is marvellous, and its price above all other fiddles ; yet there remains still one more thing which must be mentioned—its tone. It would be imagined that after such a long period of dumbness the "Messie's" utterance would be thick and stiff, speech must surely be difficult to this fairy-like thing after its century or more of silence. Nothing of the sort. When Monsieur Vuillaume's son-in-law, Alard, took his bow and loosened the Messie's long-imprisoned soul, it answered in tones more mellow, more clear, and more exquisite than a Strad that had been throbbing and pulsating for years.

In fact this wonderful fiddle has given a direct denial to the rooted opinion that mellowness and beauty of tone come from the constant vibrations of sound-waves through the pores of the wood. Its evidence seems to have brought out two facts plainly : first, that a violin is made more excellent by age (provided it is a good violin in the first place) ; and secondly, that the rushing of sound-waves through the pores of the wood is not a necessary part of its perfecting.

A FEW OTHER ITALIAN FIDDLE-
MAKERS OF NOTE

G

CHAT IV.

BERGONZI, Carlo, Cremona, 1716-1747. Best pupil of Antonius Stradivarius. His violins clearly show the teaching of the great master. They are beautiful both in form and tone, and are better preserved than most instruments of their age, owing to their massive construction. His first work was in imitation of Stradivarius, but later his genius marked out a pattern for himself. His varnish is thick, sometimes of a deep, rich, red colour; sometimes a pale red, and often a rich amber. Carlo Bergonzi lived next door to Stradivarius, setting up a business of his own about twenty years before his master's death.

His son and grandsons were also fiddle makers, and continued his business until

about 1840, when Benedetto, the last of
the fiddle-making Bergonzies, died. Carlo was
the first and best fiddle-maker of his family.

CAPPA, Geoffredo, Cremona, 1590-1640.
A pupil of Nicolo Amati, who set up in
business for himself in Piedmont. He
worked on the Amati pattern, and many of
his fiddles bear a striking resemblance to those
of his masters. The labels of his instruments
have been so tampered with that scarcely a
Cappa fiddle has its right name inside. He
was one of the best second-class Italian
makers of his time.

GAGLIANO, Alessandro, Naples, 1695-1730.
Another pupil of Antonius Stradivarius, and
the first member of a large family of fiddle-
makers. The chances of success in Cremona,
where Strad was a shining light, being small,
Gagliano, like many of the master's other
pupils, migrated to Naples. Here he seems
to have kept the field so well, that no other
makers had a chance in Naples during his
lifetime.

Gagliano's two sons, Germanio and Nicolo,
also followed their father's calling.

His model is a large, flat one. The varnish

is a yellowy-brown and very transparent.
Gagliano's cutting of his scrolls was weak and
diminutive in size.

Until a very recent date his descendants
still existed in Naples, but their work had no
great merit, and again it was the founder of
the family who was the best.

GOBBETTI, Francesco, Venice, 1690-1715.
Supposed to be another talented pupil of
Antonius Stradivarius, who migrated to
Venice. No maker has suffered more from
the practice so common some years ago, of
removing the label and inserting another
bearing a name which would be likely to
command a higher price. His model bears a
great resemblance to Stradivarius : the wood
used is handsome ; the varnish of a pale red
colour is excellent ; the tone combines both
power and sweetness.

GRANCINO, Paolo, Milan, 1665-1692. A
pupil and follower of Nicolo Amati. His
earlier fiddles are plainly copies of Amati,
but later he follows more the dictates
of his own fancy. The manner of cutting
his scrolls shows much decision. The wood
is handsome ; the varnish is a rich yellow ;
the tone is sweet, but not very powerful.

His son, Giovanni (1694-1720) was a better workman, and used finer materials than his father. His model is flatter, and the tone more powerful; varnish also yellow.

GRANCINO, Giovanni Battista, Milan, 1690. Son of Giovanni and imitator of his father. The next and last generation of Grancino inherited none of the talents of their predecessors.

GUADAGNINI, Lorenzo, Cremona, 1695-1740. Another pupil of Antonius Stradivarius, who, however, remained in Cremona, trusting that some of his master's shining light might fall on his shoulders. His fiddles are bold in design; in his sound-holes he seems to have been influenced by Guiseppe Guarnerius (son of Andrea). The model is flat, the scroll original, the varnish fairly brilliant. The tone is mellow and powerful. His instruments are ever increasing in value.

His son, Giovanni Battista, born 1711, was trained in Cremona by his father, and afterwards worked at Picenza and Parma, in which latter place he became instrument maker to the Duke. This best maker of the Guadagnini family prided himself on avoiding all imitation; however, his violins bear

resemblance to the Stradivarius model.   His
wood is most handsome, the varnish very
transparent and brilliant in colour.   Count
Cozio di Salabue, in a letter to Vincenzo
Lancetti in 1823, says: " The instruments
of G. B. Guadagnini were highly esteemed by
connoisseurs and professional men in Holland
and Germany."

Representatives of the Guadagnini family
still exist and make fiddles in Turin at the
present day.

GUARNERIUS, Andrea, 1630 - 1695.   A
pupil of Nicolo Amati, who worked side
by side with Antonio Stradivari.   He afterwards taught the art of violin-making to
his son Joseph, who carried on his father's
business after his death, and is considered
to have been the master of his cousin, the
famous Joseph Guarnerius del Gesù.

Andrea made good fiddles, but he never
attained the finish of Amati.   His son Joseph
was the most talented of the two, and showed
more originality in his models.   He seems to
have been influenced by the work of the great
Brescian master, Gasparo di Salo, and most
particularly shows it in his pointed $f\!f$ holes,
which are quite a revival of the Brescian

master's style. The varnish is thick and
rich, and the wood used generally handsome.

GUARNERIUS, Joseph del Gesù, 1683-1745.
This great fiddle-maker is the only one who
may be said to have rivalled Stradivarius.
According to Monsieur Vuillaume, Joseph del
Gesù's father was Giovanni Battesta (brother
of Andrea) and his mother was Angela Maria
Locatelli. He was born in Cremona, 8th
June 1683, and baptized on the 11th in the
Chapel of Ease of the Cathedral in the parish
of St Donato.

Unlike the rest of the family, Guarnerius'
father seems to have had nothing to do with
fiddle-making, or known anything about it,
and his son is supposed to have been placed
in his cousin Joseph's (son of Andrea) workshop to learn the fiddle-making art.

'The masterly genius of the mighty Joseph
del Gesù prevented him from ever being a
copyist, if his instruments can be said to bear
the least resemblance to any maker, old
Gasparo da Salo, the Brescian, may be quoted
as the type.

No other fiddle-maker has made such
grandiose instruments as del Gesù. His eye
for boldness of effect, and his supreme and

masterly carelessness carried him far away
from commonplace methods. Had he come
before the Amati's and Stradivarius instead
of after, Guarnerius' rugged genius would
have lead the art of lutherie in Italy. But
unfortunately he lived at a time when the
sweet but weak Amati was courted far
and near. Guarnerius hated gentleness; he
turned away from the sensitive Amati, and
chose opposite methods, like the poor
sculptor who modelled grand devils because
he was sick of fashioning saints. He was
tired of sentiment: power was his aim and
he sought it with an intensity that was often
rough, but always most lovable. To attain
his end he made many grotesque experiments; sometimes he cut the sound-holes
almost perpendicularly, often too short or too
long; frequently the wood was too thick all
over, and nothing shows his "don't care"
dash more than his massively powerful
scrolls. As to varnishing, he was a king!
he painted it on with such a smooth, feathery
touch that the most delicate grain of the
wood shows up superbly.

Guarnerius has frequently been "hauled
over the coals" for carelessness of workmanship and negligence in primary details, but

it has also been acknowledged that he could, and did, make fiddles which for their graceful boldness, handsome wood and superb varnish are unrivalled.

Among his "Violins de Luxe," which are brilliant rivals of Strad's "Messie," "Alard," or "Pucelle" are: the "Violin de Diable," (1734) deriving its name from an opera of that title in which it was played upon by its owner Saint Leoni; Monsieur Alard's superb fiddle, now in the Museum of the Paris Conservatorie; Vieuxtemp's (now Mons. Maurice Sons') fine fiddle; Emile Saurets', and last, but by far the greatest, Paganini's treasured Guarnerius, which he left to his native town of Genoa.

Paganini and Guarnerius! mighty "Gog and Magog"! The Fates for once were kind, and smilingly made the one for the other. Guarnerius built his great fiddles unnoticed and unacknowledged during his lifetime. Paganini took the neglected work, and through his genius raised it to such a pinnacle of fame that the rage for Guarnerius' fiddles continues to this day, their value varying from £200 to £400, according to condition.

The manner of Paganini's becoming

possessed of his Guarnerius is one of the
many romantic and triumphant episodes of
his life. Early in his career he was engaged
to play at a concert at Leghorn, but having
previously gambled his violin away he was
without a fiddle to play upon. "*Que
faire!*" he was *desolé* and in despair when
his good angel appeared in the shape of a
French merchant named Livron, who took
pity on him and came to his assistance by
sending him his own superb Guarnerius.

After the concert Paganini essayed to
return the instrument ᾽ to its owner, but
nothing would induce Monsieur Livron to
receive it, for, he said, his fingers could
never profane the strings which the great
artist had touched. "*C'est à vous main-
tenant que mon violin appartient;*" and
ever after the grand Guarnerius accompanied
Paganini in all his journeys.

In his will he left it to his native town
of Genoa, where it may now be seen, nestling
in soft satin beneath a canopy of glass, in
the Sala Rossa of the Municipo. On a
shelf below is placed the red leather case,
on the lid of which is stamped in plain
gold letters "*Nicolo Paganini.*" It is lined
with red plush and a bow and a packet of

coiled strings secured by the Municipal seals are placed within.

On his deathbed Paganini clasped this, his treasured Guarneri, to his breast for the last time. Since then it has only been out of its case in the Sala Rossa four times: on one occasion Camillio Sivori, Paganini's favourite pupil, was allowed to play upon it at the reception of the Duc d'Aostas, and on another Mr Edward Heron Allen, after much manœuvring with the Municipal authorities, was allowed the exquisite pleasure of examining it, playing on it, and photographing it. By his permission I insert his interesting and minute description of the proceeding.

"To write the necessary official letters, to engage a photographer, and lay in a stock of writing materials were the work of three minutes, and a procession formed itself to go and take the fiddle from its case. The procession consisted of: first, two gorgeous beadles, then the present writer, and behind him Signor Giovanni de Sonioni (Capo Ufficio del Civico Economato), and Signor Gaetano Corsi (Vice Segretario del Municipio). The procession advanced through the Sala del Consiglio through a crowd which parted right and left for us, into the Sala Rossa, where my first visit had been paid. But what a change! The whilom deserted room was lined with gaily dressed people, a triangular table stood in the middle with four armchairs in front of it, and one large one behind it. As 'our procession' entered the room an official girt in a civic scarf motioned me towards one of the armchairs. *Cielo!* the horrible situation burst upon me like a flash of lightning. *It was a civic wedding going on, and they took me for the bridegroom!* Never did harmless commissioner find himself in so ghastly a predicament, and never did he so narrowly escape an awful calamity. The necessary explanations ensued, and the society which had doubtless been relieved by this slight *divertimento*, relapsed into the normal condition of wedding-day boredom. The 'procession' having taking the violin, case, and all from the cupboard, retired in the same order in which it had advanced, reinforced by a third, larger, and more gorgeous beadle who carried the Paganini violin. Arrived in a third room, where my photographer was awaiting us, the seals of

the glass-case were solemnly broken, the
case was opened, and the fiddle, for the
first time since the death of Paganini, was
placed in the hands of a stranger.

" . . . The operations of examining the fiddle
and taking its photo occupied about three
hours, and I am inclined to regard them as
some of the most privileged moments of
my life. All the time the officials sat and
glared at me, horrified, no doubt, at the
idea that *their* fiddle should be touched by
the hands of the impious alien, whilst two
clerks drew up a *procés-verbal* of the pro-
ceedings, which we all subsequently solemnly
signed.

"The violin is of the grandest pattern of
Joseph Guarnerius del Gesù, and bears the
date 1742. The general tone of the varnish
is dark red, and it is much worn on the side
of the tailpiece where the *virtuoso's* chin
clasped it; the wood also at the edge of
the incurved side nearest the E string is
much worn away by the rapid action of the
bow in high passages. A similar, but not
so accentuated wear is found on the opposite
nearest the G string, whilst a curious deep
groove is worn right into the wood all along
the right-hand side of the finger-board. The

wear is also very marked to the right of the
neck, where the hand is placed in high
positions. The bridge, which I am assured
is the original one, is rather low, plainly cut,
and with remarkably small and thin feet.
The glorious quality of the varnish of this
unique instrument is best seen by looking
at the sides, which are in a fine state of
preservation save at the bottom and at the
right of the neck, where the varnish cannot
help 'going' on a much used fiddle.   The
back is worn with a great round wear at
the bottom of the lower curves, where the
fiddle was clasped to the master's breast;
and a circular wear in the centre of the back
shows that he was in the habit of putting
it down anywhere, and not scrupulously
returning it to its case.   To the left of this
round wear is, alas! a little patch where the
varnish has been torn off when the municipal
seal, which, at first stuck here on the
back, was afterwards removed and placed
upon the scroll, where it is comparatively
harmless.   The edges, save at the top and
bottom, are perfectly strong and unworn.
The back, which is made in two pieces, as
in the generality of fine violins, is carved
out of the most magnificent maple.   The

head of the violin, which has been fitted to
the instrument with a new neck, is very
finely cut, and has those deep grooves carved
round the scroll which the French call *les
coulisses de la tête* finely chiselled, and the
varnish here is caked in layers, which show
all its richness ; strange to say, the head has
not been much worn by turning round the
scroll, where it generally shows wear; but
the back of the head is almost worn flat,
another evidence of its having lain about
on tables and so on when not in use. The
'chin' of the scroll is very much pointed,
and the 'nut' over which the strings pass
to the bridge is made of ivory. I have been
thus minute in my description of the *wear*,
as it affords us such an insight into Paganini's
manner of playing. The patch by the side
of the tailpiece and the large wear on the
back tell of the force with which he held the
instrument so as to be able to run his hand
up the finger-board, and actually lean it
upon the instrument in those high and
pizzicato passages, which account for the
long groove down the side of the finger-
board and the broad patch at the side of
the neck, on the table of the instrument.
The wearing away of the edges in the

curves of the instrument bears a striking testimony to the force with which he sawed the gut in his *bravura* passages on the first and fourth strings. Indeed, one has only to look at the fantastic patches of exposed wood here and there upon the fiddle to conjure up the ghostly fingers that wore them bare, and the grotesque figure which it completed.

"Attached to the head of the instrument by red, white, and green ribbons, and the seal of municipality, is a card bearing the seal of Baron Achille Paganini, and the words 'Violino di Nicolo Paganini,' in his handwriting. A bow, the one he always used, stands with the violin beneath the crystal dome. The length of the whole fiddle is 60 cm., that of the body 35½ cm., from neck to rest.

"The following document is attached to the holder of the instrument: 'Genova: il quattro Luglio Mille otte cento cinquant uno. Cartolina anessa al violino del fu' Barone Nicola (*sic*) Paganini, firmata da tutte le parti intervenute nell' atto della consigna del violino medesimo, fatto in questro gioino à rogito del Notaro Giacome

Borsotto pure sottos-critto.' Then followed fourteen signatures, and the seal of the municipal arms.

"With this document there is also beneath the case a gold medal exhibited, bearing on the *obverse* the arms of Genoa, and the words 'Ordo Decur. Genu'; and on the *reverse* the legend 'Nic. Paganino Fidicini cui nemo par fuit civique bene merenti Amd cccxxxiii I.' This medal was (it will be observed) struck six years before the death of Paganini.

"I cannot now go into the many incidents in the life of this fiddle, which have been handed down to us by such historians as Fetis, Vidal, and Fleming, how it was once nearly left at an inn by his servant, and the touching story of Paganini's agony of mind when in 1836 it had to undergo a thorough repair. It was on this occasion that Vuillaume made the celebrated copy which Camillo Sivori received as a present from Paganini, and which he has played upon all his life, whether in public or private.

"On the day following the events recorded above, the duties of my mission called me away from Genoa, and I went to take one

farewell look at the fiddle in whose company
I had spent three anxious but ecstatic hours.
The door of the safe was locked and secured
with three huge seals, and in answer to my
look of enquiry and startled query, the
custodian replied:

"'The violin does not exhibit itself. An
English milor had it under observation
during yesterday, and it has been here
enclosed by His Excellency Il Sindaco,
until the English milor shall have gone away
from the *città*. They are always causing
disturbances, these English!'"

Guarnerius, like most great makers, has
been extensively copied both honestly and
dishonestly; his most successful imitators
were Carlo Ferdinando Landolfi (1750),
whose fiddles are most handsome; Lorenzo
Storioni (Cremona, 1769-1799), who made
the Guarneri model his idol; and Carlo
Guiseppe Testore (Milan, 1690-1720), who
copied him very closely.

The dishonest imitations are very numerous
and universally rough. They are generally
sold as " Prison Fiddles," taking their name
from the fable that gay young Joseph was
once imprisoned for some of his peccadillos,

and, finding favour with the jailer's daughter,
she is said to have supplied him with wood
and varnish. Judging from the existing
number of " Prison Fiddles " Joseph del Gesù
must have been incarcerated the whole of
his life.

MONTAGANA, Domenico, Cremona and
Venice, 1700-1740. A talented pupil of
Antonius Stradivarius. He worked for a
short time in Cremona after leaving his
master's workshop, and later removed to
Venice.

Most of the Italian violin-makers in those
days adopted some sign by which their
house might be easily remembered and
recognised, and their choice of a name,
as a rule, was mostly made from amongst
the Calendar of Saints. Montagana, however, boldly left the Calendar of Saints
well alone, and adopted " Cremona " as his
sign.

This maker has also suffered severely
from the wicked habit of false labelling.
Many a fine fiddle labelled Bergonzi or
Andrea Guarneri, is really the grand
work of this " mighty Venetian." Mr Hart
says :

"Montagana was in every way original,
but the fraud that foisted his works upon
makers who were better known, has prevented his name from being associated with
many of his choicest instruments."

He continues to say that the merits of
Montagana and Carlo Bergonzi are:

"Daily more appreciated, and when the
scarcity of their genuine work is considered,
it becomes a matter of certainty that their
rank must be raised to the point indicated,
viz., that of Amati and Stradivarius."

RUGGIERI, Francesco, Cremona, 1668-1720.
A member of a large family of fiddle-
makers, but little inferior in position to the
Amati family. His work is of the Amati
type. His instruments are very graceful
in outline, and the varnish difficult to
surpass. His son, Grancinto, followed his
father's trade also. Till about 1723 the
Ruggieri's lived in Cremona.

SERAFINO SANTO, Udine, Venice, 1710-
1748. His fiddles strongly resemble both the
Amati and the Stainer model. Their chief

attractions are the handsome and exquisite finish of his workmanship.

He branded his name on nearly all his instruments, just above the tail pin.

GERMAN MAKERS

CHAT V.

GERMAN MAKERS—JACOBUS STAINER.
Born 14th July 1621, died 1683.

To Jacobus Stainer of Absam in the Tyrol,
the German "Geigenmacher" owes a debt
of eternal gratitude for establishing the true
era of violin-making in that country. Unlike
sunny Italy, where this beautiful art had
commenced to flourish more than twenty
years previously, Germany in the first half
of the seventeenth century still adhered to
the sweet old viols. She cared nothing for
the whispered murmurs of the new Italian
invention called "Il Violino," or its makers,
Amati, da Salo, Maggini, but recurrently
chiselled and ornamented her bulky children
in frugal happiness.

Suddenly like a bolt from the blue came
native Jacobus Stainer, who, regardless of
all tradition, strode through the mists of

the woods, tapping the hearts of the tall, gentle trees and cutting unknown paths for his fellow-countrymen.

This "father of the German fiddle" was born in the little village of Absam in the Tyrol, 14th July 1621, exactly twenty-three years before Antonius Stradivarius in Cremona. How he attained the knowledge of his art is quite unknown; without foundation his genius appears to have thriven and grown strong on the principle of Topsy, the nigger wench, who:

"Nebber was born, and nebber had a mudder,
Spec she grow'd a nigger child jus like any udder.'

Nor is anything definitely known of his father or mother, except that the first rejoiced in the name of Martin, the second in Sabine Grafinger, and that they had three sons, Paul, who was a master-joiner, Mark, who migrated to Austria and made fiddles in that country, and the brilliant but unfortunate Jacobus.

In his youth Stainer doubtless had opportunities of seeing some of the Amati fiddles in use at the Court of the Archduke Leopold at Innsbruck. The sight of them may have roused his dormant passion for the graceful thing : but, although, he observed and watched, he stood aside with folded arms, never attempting to copy. To him the tone of the Italian violin was not altogether pleasing, so he "thought and thought, and worked and worked, and thus created the German violin."

Stainer commenced his deep reflections at such an early age, that at twenty he was already making saleable fiddles, which were purchased by strangers at the Absam markets. For these embryo conceptions he received six florins, about the same sum as we pay now for a cheap new fiddle.

About two years later he made a successful visit to the neighbouring town of Salzburg, and shortly after became acquainted with Margaret Holzhammer, a lady three years younger than himself, whom he married in 1645.

At this period of his life poor Stainer's ducats could not have been numerous, for after his marriage he ignominiously lived with his wife's parents. Then he and his family became most unsettled, leading the comfortless existence of inhabiting various houses in Absam. This sort of preambulation eventually got on Stainer's nerves, and one fine morning, in 1648, he rashly turned his back on Absam, and tried his fiddle-making luck at Kirchdorf in Austria.

Here he remained a short time, lodging in the house of a Jew merchant, Solomon Huebner, whose acquaintance he made on his departure from Hall. In after years this gentleman was the *bête noir* of unfortunate Stainer's life; like a sword of Damocles, the Jew merchant and his ever-increasing debt hung over the poor fiddle-maker's head.

Returning from Kirchdorf in debt to Huebner, Stainer had the good fortune to attract the attention of the Archduke Charles Ferdinand, who, with his wife, the Grand Duchess of Tuscany, and whole court, stayed for a short time near Hall. During the Archducal visit he was allowed both to exhibit and play on his fiddles before the Court, and found so much favour that he received by Diploma the title of "Hofgeigen-macher" to his Highness.

Now came the most successful period of his life; he took up his quarters near the Archducal Palace, successfully working there until 1656, when he actually bought a house, with a garden attached, from his father-in-

law. Facing Krupp Castle, his new abode
was situated on the main road, and sheltered
on one side by stately lindens. The house
still exists though the tall lindens have been
cut down.

Here name and fame at last were his.
His full title became that of "most celebrated
maker of stringed instruments," with the
addition of "Ersamer mich fürnchmer Herr"
(honourable and excellent).

Now flocked pupils anxious to learn from
so distinguished a master of the art; and all
the way from Mittenwald in Bavaria, where,
"Was the German Cremona for fiddle-
making or, as it was first called, lute-making,
came a young man called Kloz to learn of
Stainer in Absam, and then returned to his
native place. He was a worthy pupil, Kloz
taught his son Matthias, and so founded a
branch which is still flourishing."

Matthias Albani, of Bozen, was also a pupil
and imitator of this master.

In 1662 Stainer's patron, the Archduke,
died, and was succeeded by the unmusical
Sigismund Francis, who did away with all
music, dismissed the Court musicians, poor
Stainer amongst them.

Again evil days fell upon this unfortunate

man. Huebner, from Kirchdorf, began to
clamour for payment; poor Stainer contrived
to send about fifteen guelden and gave an
I.O.U. for the rest, to be paid at the
approaching Hall yearly market. Alas! this
I.O.U. he was unable to reclaim, so the
Shylock Huebner took the matter into court;
the judge happily sided with Stainer, and
some temporary arrangement was agreed to.

About the same time Stainer was accused
of Lutheranism and imprisoned, through
which terrible misfortune he lost nearly all
his noble patrons. When released on
27th September 1669, the respite from his
trials only lasted a few months, for the
wretched Huebner worried him more and
more, the debt in some mysterious way
having in the meantime increased instead of
grown smaller.

In 1672 he strove with great energy to
regain his former position, and, going to
Salzburg, received from the treasury
seventy-two gueldens for a Viola da Gamba
(bass viol) and two Viola da Braccio (small
viols). About this time he made some
magnificent fiddles, but was dragged back
again through being sued for a debt of
450 guelden.

Clutching at the last straw, Stainer petitioned the Emperor for a return of his former favours. But the Emperor turned a deaf ear to his entreaties (on account of the Lutheran episode). This blow was the last and greatest, for on receipt of the bad news, in 1678, poor Stainer ceased working, fell into a melancholy state, finally became mad, and died in the greatest poverty in 1683.

After his death, Stainer's house was purchased by his brother-in-law, Blasius Keil, and his unfortunate widow and eight daughters became homeless wanderers. Six years later his unhappy wife died in the greatest poverty, and shortly after two daughters died poor and unmarried.

In spite of the cruel blows of fate which pursued Stainer throughout his life, his powerful gifts repeatedly reasserted themselves; great thoughts came to him like instincts, and raised his work to a high standard of perfection. Had he been free to utilise his powers, *sans gêne* his work would have been more universally good; but the debts, the religious troubles, and the compulsory need of providing for his family often forced him to hurry his work.

His earlier instruments were unsettled in

model and small in size, the _ff_ holes long
and narrow, the belly high built, the wood
coarse-fibred, the varnish of a clear, dark,
reddish colour.   After a time when his
fiddles became better known, and he commanded higher prices, he used much finer
grained wood ; this he fetched himself from
beyond Salzburg.

Stainer's choice of timber was quite
remarkable ; frequently he spent days in
the woods searching for a suitable tree,
wandering past oaks and beeches till he
lighted on a pine.   Then, before felling it,
he always tapped it with his hammer, to
ascertain its acoustical powers.   If the tree
answered with the right resonance, out would
come the trusty axe and do its heartless
work of destruction.   Often he would make
a point of being present when some stately
tree was being felled on a high summit,
so as to hear the tone it gave in its mad
bound from rock to rock.

Stainer's rarest fiddles are those made
about 1644.   These were small, high-built
instruments, and contained autograph labels
Vuillaume's son-in-law, Alard, is said to have
possessed an elegant fiddle of this period,
and the Duc d'Orleans (grandfather of King

Louis Phillipe) also owned a fine specimen. In 1817 this instrument, for which he paid 3500 florins in 1771, passed into the hands of Viotti's pupil, Monsieur Cartier. One exceptionally good-toned Stainer, dated 1653, and bearing his autograph lable, was made by him for the Hall Cathedral. From there it went to the Hall Parish Church where it was used in the choir. Its tone was so rich that it could be heard above the full orchestra. Mozart possessed a Stainer which he held in high esteem and often played on. This also bore Stainer's autograph, and was dated 1656. Remis, the Belgian violinist, had a beautiful Stainer of a later date, given him by the Empress Maria Theresa.

Though not so piercing as the Italian violins, the tone of Stainer's fiddles is remarkably gentle and flute-like. Monsieur Savart, whose experiments have thrown much light on the acoustical methods of the ancient fiddle-makers, once tested a Stainer fiddle; he selected one of his most valued violins and a Stainer, and invited two excellent violinists to play upon them side by side. After a thorough trial, he gave the preference to the Stainer, con-

I

sidering it to be far superior. Monsieur
Vuillaume, after hearing Paganini's pupil,
Sivori, play on a Stainer, was also greatly
struck with its wonderful and sympathetic
quality of tone. Both Savart's and
Vuillaume's opinions are highly flattering to
Stainer, but the most thorough appreciation
of Stainer's fiddles, was offered by the renowned Count Von Trantmannsdorf. Here
is the romantic story.

In 1756 Count Wenzel of Trantmannsdorf,
Master of the Horse to the Emperor Charles
VI., once received the honour of a visit
from that monarch, accompanied by King
Frederick William of Prussia, and other
princes. He was most lavish in his expenditure, among other things engaging
the well-known Faustina and her companion, Mauro Allesi, to perform before
his Royal guests.

At this time Prince Wenzel of Lichtenstein
was sent as ambassador for the Emperor
Charles VI., to the Court of France, and
he asked Count Von Trantmannsdorf to
allow him to take with him the two famous
virtuosi, George and his brother Nicholas
Stezitsky, then in Von Trantmannsdorf's
service. The latter consented. Now

George Stezitsky was only provided with
an inferior violin; Mauro Allesi, on the
other hand, had brought with him several
Cremona fiddles, and, when called upon
by the Count with a more than "countly"
offer, to supply one for George Stezitsky,
he would in no wise consent. Thereupon
the Count dismissed him with fifty ducats,
and Faustina with a thousand guelden.
While the Count was still in a state of
embarrassment as to where to procure a
fiddle, a very aged master presented himself and played so excellently on a Stainer
fiddle, that in the minds of the Royal
guests and of all connoisseurs, the remem-
brance of the Cremona fiddles was entirely
eclipsed.

The Count at once decided to purchase
this fiddle, and for that purpose interrupted
the player, who, under the apprehension
that he had not made a good impression,
was quite beside himself with dismay. When
the Count tried to soothe him and gave him
to understand that he wished to acquire
the fiddle, the old man replied that if he
were to lose the fiddle he would also lose
his art and his good fortune, because he did
not know how he would be able to earn

his livelihood in the future without it. Hearing this, the Count gave him first, for playing, fifty ducats; then came to the following terms: three hundred guelden for the fiddle yearly, a suit of clothes, daily board, daily one measure of wine plus two casks of beer, free housing, wood, light; then monthly, ten guelden, and yearly, six bushels of fruit, and finally as many hares as he required for his kitchen.

After this bargain George Stezitsky had to play a solo on the violin, and later the Count presented it to him.

The man who had given up his violin on the above conditions lived sixteen years, and thus received out of the Count's funds:

	fl.	kr.
Ready money for the fiddle . .	300	0
As a present	100	0
Monthly, 10 fl.	1,920	0
Daily board at 20 kr. . . .	1,946	40
100 fr. yearly for suit . . .	1,600	0
Measure of wine daily, 12 kr. .	1,168	0
Yearly, 800 measures beer at 4 kr.	853	20
Yearly, 6 bush. fruit at 3 fl. . .	288	0
Daily, 6 "klafter" of wood at 3 fl.	288	0
Light daily, 1 krz.	97	20
For four years after his death his cousin received 6 bush. fruit .	72	0

	fl.	kr.
And after her an old widow received ½ klafter of *wood* and 4 fl. house rent	22	0
The same, also received monthly, 1 fl. 30 kr. and furthermore okr.	78	0
This makes a sum of . . .	8,733	20
And according to the 24 fl.— standard—10, ...	380	24

At George Stezitsky's death many wanted the violin, but the then owner would not sell, not wishing to incur the displeasure of Count von Trantmannsdorf.

On Trantmannsdorf's death it was bought by the Hofmusckus, Zart of Prussia. At Zart's death it passed into possession of Fränzel, Conzertmeister in Munich. Later this violin passed through many hands, belonging at one time to Herr Chronsel, of Vienna, who, in 1854, lent it for a few hours in order to enhance the festivities at the marriage of the Emperor of Austria. This is the last time this fiddle was played on in public.

Stainer in his lifetime gained much renown, but since his death his fame has been tarnished by later fiddle-makers affixing *his* name to their very ordinary instruments.

This and the fact that the Absam master was a slow worker renders his authentic work scarce and valuable.

A Pilgrimage to the House of Jacob Stainer.

A journey having a definite object is wont to be playfully termed a pilgrimage, but this journey—let this be clearly understood and accounted to me for grace—is *really* a pilgrimage, for, in the year A.D. 1797, in a house only a stone's-throw from that in which Stainer "lived his art" (as the quaint phraseology of the tablet on his house hath it), a picture of the Holy Virgin miraculously appeared one fine summer morning. One can imagine an immediate sequence of occurrences similar to those recorded by Mr Hewlett in his "Madonna of the Peach Tree"—the scared but withal delighted peasants, the pious joy not wholly untainted with more practical considerations of the parish priests, and the proprietary airs of the mayor and corporation, supposing so remote a hamlet as Absam in the Austrian Tyrol to possess such dignitaries; sufficeth for this present narrative that the

house became the "Müttergottes Haus,"
the picture was removed to the church,
which had only recently been degraded
from the grace of its original Gothic design
to its present barn style of architecture by
the lack of taste then prevailing, and
pilgrims were invited to visit the shrine.
Since then the invitation has been readily
responded to, and a steady stream of devout
Tyrolese, year in and year out, treads the Via
Crucis which winds through the hayfields
from Breitweg, decorated with barbarously
executed Stations of the Cross.

The number of violinists who, on their
way to or from Ober Ammergau this year,
turn aside to visit the home of "the father
of the German fiddle" (I quote the tablet
once more) is conjectural. Judging from
my own experience, I should say none.
And yet the journey is well worth its
trouble—for that it takes some trouble (from
the point of view of the hurrying tourist
with an inexorable programme) cannot be
denied.

We are at Innsbruck, most Italian of
Austrian towns, and thence a steam railway
takes us in three-quarters of an hour to
Hall-in-Tyrol. From the Stadplatz, a wind-

ing and precipitous street, paved with un-
compromising boulders, leads up and up to
the Pfarrkirche, most *baroque* of Tyrolese
churches, where the skeleton of one whole
saint—St Fortunatus—decked in unspeak-
able tinsel and improbable jewellery, sleeps
in a glass box, and the skulls and isolated
bones of a hundred other saintly persons
repose behind glass in the Lady Chapel.
The efficacy of these "confused relics" (to
quote Mr Harvey) is testified by innumerable
wax models of eyes, ears, noses, mouths,
arms, legs, and whole babies, that hang in
festoons upon every available inch of wall
space. The spectacle is at once gruesome
and pathetic. Climbing ever upwards past
the church, we reach the dilapidated hamlet
of Breitweg, where the main thoroughfares
furnish a farmyard for whosoever cares to
turn his livestock into them, and thence,
across acres of hayfield gemmed with every
conceivable flower in carpets of many tinted
loveliness, we reach the outskirts of Absam,
where bowers of roses compete with the
tanneries which "turn the live air sick."
Here we are at the Pfarrkirche, which is
surrounded by booths for the sale of votive
tablet and taper, of rosaries and manuals of

devotion, the libretti, so to speak, of the
miracle, and of the illustrated post card
which every German tourist must despatch
to his distant friends from whatever spot
wherein he finds himself resting for five
minutes. Past the church and some little
distance up the village street, we reach the
Stainer Grasse, and, a little way up this last,
we come to a well-to-do and picturesque
châlet, standing in its own garden and courtyard, and half overgrown by a flourishing
plum-tree that springs from the south-east
corner.

On the front of this house is affixed a
tablet which bears inscription:

> In diesem Hause
> lebte seiner Kunst
> JAKOB STAINER,
> Der Vater der deutschen Geige.
> Geboren zu Absam 14 Juli 1621,
> hier gestorben 1683.

Search among the local archives has
revealed the following facts in the history
of this house. It was bought by Stainer
from one Paul Holzhammer, who was his
brother-in-law, on the 12th November 1666,
and after his death it was sold (on the

18th January 1684) for seven hundred florins
to another brother-in-law of Stainer, by
name Blasius Kiel. The house, as shown
in the accompanying view, was restored and
to some extent reconstructed in 1820.

On the south side of the house, under
the projecting eaves, is a balcony or loggia,
on which one knows that Stainer stored
and ripened his wood, even as the present
proprietors store and dry their wood there
for building or burning. Of relics of the
great fiddle-maker the house is bereft, save
that in a room on the upper storey is
an ordinary substantial work-bench, which
we are informed was the actual bench at
which he worked — at which he "lived his
art."

And do the natives of Absam feel a proper
pride in their most celebrated compatriot?
Not at all. There is not even a post card
with a picture of his house on it to be had
in the place. To any one who knows the
Tirol this omission expresses the insignificance of this, for us, holy spot. Did the
natives but know the story of Count
Trantmannsdorf and the fancy annuities
that he is reported to have granted in
exchange for one of Stainer's fiddles, and

were these annuities but reduced to concrete expression in the hopelessly confused coinage of the district—guelden, krone, kellers, fillers, and kreutzers—one may be sure that the Stainer-haus would rank in their estimation side by side with the Müttergottes Haus, and the post card would flourish in the local shops.

I came away feeling a little sad, and also a little infected with the disease that floats in the air, for, before leaving, I sent a picture post card to Arthur Hill.

EDWARD HERON ALLEN.

INNSBRUCK, 16th June 1900.

STAINER.

BY HERMANN VON GILM.

Translated from the German by L. B.

1.

The fiddle-maker Stainer
  Goes whistling through the wood,
A master than whom finer
  You'll seek nor meet as good.

2.

He passes by tall beeches
  And oaks of ancient stem
Disdainful, what he searches
  Lives not, he knows, in *them.*

3.

But in the sunshine yonder
  From out her ivy sheath,
A pine tree seems to ponder
  O'er all that dwells beneath.

4.

And nods like chamois that in
  The distance scents mishap—
Her bodice of white satin
  With straining nigh to snap.

5.

Then fast climbs up the master
  That ivy case so sheer,
And to the bark yet faster
  Lays anxiously his ear.

6.

And taps it with his hammer
  In mingled hope and fear,
As tapped he at her chamber—
  His lady love so dear.

7.

When from within there issues
  As 'twere a gentle moan
Whose anguish through the tissues
  Of ev'ry branch is thrown.

8.

The master, nought relented ;
  Taps on in pity's scorn,
Till from that breast tormented
  A grievous cry is torn.

9.

"As swan," he shouts, "she's singing
  When piercèd to the heart,"
His sturdy axe true swinging
  His handiwork to start.

10.

Blow after blow swift dealing,
  Till, felling to the ground,
And all her splendour peeling,
  But her pale corse is found.

11.

But why go on ? for clearly
  Of all her beauty bright
Is left but wood—wood merely
  And litter for one night.

SECOND PART.

1.

Day to its close is pressing,
  When starts up from his seat
The master with a blessing—
  His fiddle is complete.

2.

He fondles it with rapture
  And taps it yet again,
His ear intent to capture
  That pure, sweet, silv'ry strain.

3.

" Now shalt thou fully prove it,
  O youngest—born of mine,
What song—to those who love it—
  Hides in our forest pine.

4.

" And prove, too, there's a miner
  In our dear land, Tyrol,
Than gneiss, salt, gold holds finer
  This, this, thy very soul."

5.

His says, nor further staying
  Reward withheld too long,
Plays, but what greets his playing
  Is no mechanic song.

6.

But living, human accents
  With tears that seem to break,
And then in wildest anger
  A sweet revenge to take.

7.

" Oh ! happy I tho' martyr'd
  All martyr'd ones among,
For hast not thou, hardhearted,
  Giv'n me thyself a tongue ?

8.

" The woodland life, the youthful,
  Thou ruin'dst in its prime,
Give back again, and, ruthful,
  Give back the dear old time,

9.

" When, after winter's slumbers,
  In ev'ry vein I knew
Sweet spring—and countless numbers
  Of songbirds round me flew.

10.

" When round my head in daytime
  The gentle breeze would creep,
And at my feet in night-time
  The anemone would sleep.

11.

" Give back the joy of living,
  The array thou would'st not spare,
The body that in sunlight,
  Chaste sunlight, thou could'st bare.

12.

" The soul, thou sayest, Master,
    The soul, and naked too—
Learn, fool, to thy disaster,
    Thy heartless touch to rue ! "

13.

On, on he plays till dawning,
    And o'er the heav'ns are spread
The earliest clouds of morning
    All tipp'd with rosy red.

14.

Till with last ray of reason
    And tott'ring he all o'er,
The fiddle firm he seizes
    And dashes to the floor.

15.

The sun mounts high and higher
    In all his glory bright,
But leaves alas ! poor Stainer
    In madness' darkest night.

Something about French and English Makers.

According to Mr Hart the birth of the
violin took place both in France and England
in the early part of the seventeenth century.
François Medard and the old viol maker,
Tywersus, were the pioneers in France, and
Rayman and Wise in England. These two
nations unanimously copied the Italian

models until the beginning of the eighteenth century, when England, being attracted by the glamour of Jacobus Stainer, whose fame was then at its height, adopted this model, and continued to copy the distinguished German until the middle of the same century. Then Benjamin Bank's talent was the means of turning the tide in favour of the Italian model once again.

Among the best French makers were Bouquay, Paris (1700-1730); he copied the Amati fiddles. Augustine Chappy (1711); de Comble, a pupil of Stradivarius. Fendt, who although a German, may be classed amongst French makers as he lived and worked entirely in Paris between 1765 and 1780. He copied the Strad model with much finish.

In 1794, Nicholas, the most talented of the Lupot family, settled in Paris, and exercised his exceptional gifts also in copying Stradivarius. Lupot's instruments are beautifully finished, and their tone improve immensely year by year. His fiddles are now worth about £200 or more. As a repairer he was both skilful and noted. Spohr was a great admirer of Lupot, and played on one of his instruments for years.

Contemporary with Nicholas Lupot was Pique, who ran Lupot very closely. It is said there was much rivalry between the two makers, and poor Pique has been accused of buying Lupot's fiddles unvarnished, putting on his own coat of varnish, and labelling them as his own. Pique was, however, individually a very clever maker.

The nineteenth century boasted much talent. There was the distinguished Chanot family, who so faithfully copied both Stradivarius and Guarnerius, that the inexperienced eye cannot detect the difference; and François Chanot's pupil, the great Jean Baptiste Vuillaume. He was the first maker to sell his copies of Strad, etc., as copies and nothing else. Vuillaume loved the great Cremona master's work and imitated him most closely, even in the matter of prodigality, for he made about three thousand fiddles, "which," he was wont to say, "were all sold, all paid for; and the money spent, and it affords one great satisfaction."

Vuillaume was intimately connected with Tarisio, from whom he bought the "Messie," and other notable fiddles. During the Commune of 1870, this instrument was in much peril, and Vuillaume wrote to his daughter, Madame Alard, in great perturbation, asking her advice as to where best to hide his precious " Messie," and various other treasures :

"In my last I spoke to you of Alard's violin and my 'Messie,' and of certain valuable articles I have here. I do not know what to do with them. If one survives one can recover the valuables when the hubbub is over ; some *sous* can be buried, but violins cannot be buried.

". . . Where ought I to place all these in case of pillage?" Poor Vuillaume! Happily he solved the problem of concealment, for later he writes: "I have found a safe hiding-place protected from fire, *et puis à la grace de Dieu !*"

Vuillaume was a great connoisseur, a skilful repairer and a notable figure amongst dealers.

Then there was Lupot's pupil, Pierre Sylestre, who was a most delicate worker, and a copyist of Stradivarius, and the Gand family, whose founder, François was another pupil of Lupot's. Gand married Nicholas Lupot's daughter, and carried on the business after Lupot's death. François Gand was a king of repairers, often accomplishing seeming impossibilities. The firm, now Gand et Bernedel, still exists in Paris.

Besides other masculine makers, more or less important, French luthiers can boast the unique honour of counting one of the fair sex among their number. This pioneer of lady violin-makers was wife of François Chanot's brother George, Florentine Demoliens. She was the sole author of three beautiful violins ; the first, made in 1827, was shown at the Exhibition of French Industries, and was the admiration of artists and amateurs ; the second was made to order for an English amateur 'cellist named Carleton ; and the third, and most interesting, was made for and presented to Viotti's pupil, Monsieur J. B. Cartier, author of the violin school, *L'Art du Violin.* On this violin Monsieur Cartier had the happy thought of causing the history of the violin to be painted, and from this the fiddle was named "Violin Historique et Monumental." The design for the painting was made by the brothers Debret—one the architect of the Church of St Dennis, and the other Court painter to the Emperor of Brazil—assisted by their nephew.

The difficult task of painting the design

on the undulating surface of the violin was undertaken by the artist Darincourt. According to Monsieur Cartier's description of the painting (which has been rewritten and preserved by Cyprien Desmarias), the picture contained representations of all the members of the violin family. Supporting the pillars of a Gothic arch were Horus, the Egyptian Apollo, playing the lyre, and Whichnon, the Indian Apollo, playing the flute. These two figures represented the sources from whence the violin has presumably sprung. Then in niches there were representations of Arnold, a celebrated professor in the time of Charlemagne, depicted playing on a five-stringed viol; this was copied from a figure surmounting the entrance to the Church of St Dennis, built in 1137: next to him, a portrait bust of Perdigon, a noted thirteenth century troubadour, and an accomplished performer on bow instruments. Gazing at Perdigon, Colin Musét, a contemporary and also celebrated troubadour, playing on a violin which in shape much resemble the form now so familiar. This figure was copied from the Church of St Julien des Ménétri, built in 1333. Then there was a representation of a wonderful fountain

found in an old ruined palace at Soissons.
On the basin were shown various players
of the harp and rebec. To illustrate the
mediæval custom of serving distinguished
guests on horseback, the mounted minstrel,
which followed and preceded the actual
server, was shown playing on a rude violin.
On a pedestal stood a Welsh bard playing
a six - stringed crouth with a bow, and
Chilperic, King of France, clothed in Royal
robes, playing on a little vielle; this was
copied from the Cathedral of Notre Dame.
Opposite Chilperic is a prince, also playing
on the vielle, taken from the Chapel of
the Church of St George of Boscherville,
built in 1066. At the bottom of the design
are two women playing on three-stringed
rebecs; and finally, the last picture, which
depicts the popular tradition connected with
the name of Pierre Sygebard, the celebrated
thirteenth century minstrel. He was represented kneeling and playing on a five-stringed
viol before Notre Dame de Rocamador. At
the head of the viol burnt a wax taper, which
the devil, disguised as a monk, repeatedly
tried to snatch away, while the crowd pressed
round the minstrel, seemingly ravished by
his songs of praise to the Virgin. Each

time the monk snatched the wax taper, it miraculously returned to the vielle of its own accord. Pierre Sygebard was dressed in long, flowing, red robes, which appear to have been the accepted costume of the thirteenth century minstrel. This remarkable violin was on view at Chanot's in 1836.

The greatest industry in French violin-making is now carried on at Mirecourt, where thousands of cheap violins are turned out yearly and sent all over the world. Here they manufacture imitation Amati's, Maggini's, da Salo's, Stradivarius', etc., with that charred appearance of age which deceives the trusting amateur, and causes him with glowing eye to purchase what he fondly imagines is "a bargain, don't you know!" At Mirecourt fiddles are made on the system of the Chicago sausage, which is a pig one moment and a nice, neat, mashed up savoury roll the next. These sham "old fiddles" greet one at every turn, and their price is from 12s. 6d. onward. The original cost of constructing them is quite a revelation to the uninitiated. According to Monsieur Lamy, the principal fiddle-maker of Mirecourt, the following is a true estimate of the cost of making the most moderate-priced violin.

	£	s	d
Wood for back	£0	0	2
„ „ belly	0	0	2
„ „ neck	0	0	1
Workmanship in neck . .	0	0	2
Blackened finger-board . .	0	0	2
Workmanship of back and belly	0	0	3
Cutting out by saw . . .	0	0	1½
Shaping back and belly by machinery	0	1	0
Varnish	0	0	10
Fitting up strings, bridge tail piece	0	0	9½
	0	3	7
6 per cent. for general expenses .	0	0	3
	0	3	10
15 per cent. profit . . .	0	0	8
	£0	4	6

.   .   .   .

The English fiddle-makers up to the last thirty years were pretty numerous. England, like the rest of the world, was not slow in pricking her ears to the rumours of the Italian viols and viol-makers. Like France, she also liked the idea, and straightway set to work constructing her wooden boxes of a like shape. But in one respect she outdid France, for, outside of being a mere copiest, she actually *lead*, and made hard and fast rules which were universally adopted.

It was she who first applied the sensitive, metal strings to those tenor and bass viols, which are now respectively known as those beautiful instruments the "Viola d'Amore" and the "Viola da Gamba," and it was she who moderated the shape and fixed the size of the viols so as to render them more adaptable to the performance of elaborate music.

Previous to her making these alterations viols were universally large, so large, we are told, that in France it was an ordinary custom to shut *un petit Page* within the viol to sing the treble part, while the player scraped out the accompaniment on the selfsame instrument.

The names of the earliest sixteenth-century makers were Aldred, Rosse, and after these Smith, Bolles, Addison, Shaw. All these makers followed the Italian models, as also did Urquhart, and his pupil Barak Norman (1688-1740). The last-named copied Maggini immensely; most of his instruments are ornamented and double purfled like those of the Brescian master.

After Barak Norman a sudden revulsion

of feeling set in for the Stainer model and English makers like a flock of sheep copied him until about 1750; then Benjamin Banks the "English Amati, foremost and most skilled of English makers, turned the tide in favour of the Italian models again.

A contemporary of Benjamin Banks was William Foster, the talented Cumberland spinning-wheel maker. He, with his son William of the same trade, occupied all their spare time in the fascinating craft of fiddle-making and fiddle-repairing. His son William came to London in 1759, and after a term of apprenticeship set up a business of his own near St Martin's Lane.

He also imitated Stainer for a short period, but later made some magnificent copies of Amati. Foster's 'cellos are particularly fine; Ludley's concert instrument was by this distinguished English maker.

Thomas Dodd is another name to which much fame is attached, he was great in the art of varnishing, and as a reason for his superiority in this respect, advertised that he possessed the receipt for the original Cremona varnish. This was a sensational mode of advertisement, but neither true nor necessary, for Dodd's varnish was all his own, and first-class. He attained a big reputation, and his excellent 'cellos commanded between £40 and £50.

Richard Duke was another excellent copyist of Stainer and Amati. Present-day makers are (to use an Irishism) chiefly repairs, the *Cheap Violin* and the genuine *Old Violin* have so monopolised the market that large firms have been compelled to relinquish any individual efforts, and content themselves by manufacturing moderate-priced copies, and repairing. Their work is every bit as good, if not better, than the old makers, but the public shudder at the mere thought of a new violin. For this "drug in the market" they are willing to pay only a very moderate price, and will only be lavish when it is a question of purchasing a real *old* fiddle.

Against these odds what is a man to do? Times have changed, the horse is superseded by the motor car; trains burrow in the earth instead of respectably rolling upon it, and all is hurry and scurry, and quick profit and restless speed. In the midst of such a medley the ancient and honoured lute-maker can find no place. His sobriety and dignity, combined with that true

artistic sense which made him regardless
of time and season alike, must of necessity
be replaced by the keen man of business
with a level head and a determination to turn
the fortunate chances of life to good account.
Alas for art!

*Description of the Construction of the Violin,
and something about its Varnish.*

A casual observer of the violin will find
it difficult to believe that such an apparently
simple instrument requires some seventy
pieces for its construction. If correctly and
mathematically adjusted each piece fulfils a
function of its own towards the perfection of
the united whole, but the minutest deviation
or lack of "balance" at any point, will utterly
destroy the fiddle.

The back.: the back is usually made
of hard maple or sycamore. Although no
special importance attaches to the methods
of cutting it, still, there are three ways: in
one piece technically termed (1) "slab back,"
cut the way of the grain; or (2) "whole
back," cut across the grain when the wood
is broad enough; or (3), as is more common,
in two pieces joined down the centre; Stradi-

varius seems to have preferred the last method.

The belly : this is made of soft, fine-grained pine or deal, from the heart of the tree ; the best comes from Switzerland, Dalmatia, and the Tyrol. It is usually split, and joined down the centre. The arching, both of belly and back, are obtained by scooping out the wood from the solid block on both sides, and *not* by bending with heat.

The sound-holes : slightly below the middle of the belly are the sound-holes. These are in the form of *f*. Their function is to allow the sound to escape from the interior of the instrument. The tone of the fiddle is influenced by the angle at which the sound-holes are placed, also by their distance apart, their shape, and their size. The farther they are apart, the sweeter the tone, and the nearer together, the louder and harsher the sound. Gasparo da Salo was the earliest Italian maker to give this definite shape to the sound-holes, and to realise its scientific value. The Amatis improved greatly on da Salo's rigid *ff*, and Stradivarius and Serafino brought their predecessors' efforts to perfection.

The purfling: this edging is inlaid, not, as might be supposed for ornamentation, but to prevent the sharp outline of the violin from being chipped. Purfling is made of strips of white maple, and strips of the same wood stained black. The white is inlaid on each side of the black strip. Either twenty-four or thirty-six strips are used, and the art of embedding these to the right depth round the edge of the violin is a most delicate one. The purfling of the Amatis has been surpassed by few makers. Some Dutch fiddle-makers (notably Jacobs) used whalebone instead of maple wood.

The ribs: these are the thin curved pieces of wood which unite the back and the belly. They are six in number, and by the application of a hot bending iron, are curved to correspond with the outline of the violin-mould. The thickness of the ribs are not uniform; they are a trifle deeper near the tail-piece. Their union with the back and belly is strengthened within by twelve strips of pine called "linings," and their six points of juncture are solidified by six pieces of carefully shaped pine called blocks.

The scroll: the scroll is the termination of the neck of the instrument. Although apparently so simple, the scroll is most difficult to carve, and has proved a stumbling block to many an accomplished fiddle-maker. Every maker has displayed his individuality in his manner of cutting his scroll. Stradivarius excelled in beauty, Guarnerius in rugged strength amounting sometimes to eccentricity, Gagliano for weakness and insignificance.

The neck: that portion of the instrument to which the ebony finger-board is attached. Made of sycamore.

The peg-box: part of the scroll through which the rose wood, ebony or boxwood pegs pass.

The tail-piece: the piece of ebony shaped like a V and pierced with holes through which the knotted ends of the gut-strings are passed and attached. The tail-piece is attached to

The tail-pin: by a stout piece of gut, and the tail-pin fits (without glue) into the bottom block on the join of the lower ribs.

The finger-board: the piece of ebony wood attached to the neck. The strings pass from the tail-piece over the bridge, and over the finger board, into the little niches for them on

The nut: and are attached to the pegs.

The bast-bar: a strip of pine, rounded on one side and attached to the under side of the belly on the left of the fiddle, tapering at each end. This is glued to the interior of the belly according to a precise mathematical calculation. Its function is to give weight to the vibrations of the low notes, and thus give them great depth and sonority.

The sound-post: a small pillar of spruce wood which stands vertically within the violin, and held in place by the pressure of the strings upon the belly. Its position is behind the right foot of the bridge.

The French call this the "soul" of the violin with much truth, for by means of this small column, the vibrations of the back, the belly, and the contained mass of air are brought into unison and equilibrium. The sound-post has to be regulated with great nicety and care, and only an expert workman understands fitting it perfectly to the shape of the back and belly.

The bridge: the bridge is made of maple. Owing to the genius of Stradivarius, we have now a perfect pattern. The cutting and fitting of the bridge also require an expert workman.

The varnish.· is the last word in scientific fiddle-making. Its functions are (1) to preserve the wood of the instrument from the ravages of time; (2) to impart beauty to the finished fiddle; and (3) to cause fiddle-makers and theorists to fight with one another, and write to the papers, musical and otherwise. "The Secret of the Cremona Varnish" (this is generally the heading of the letters above referred to) lies in the fact that it never was any secret at all. The Cremonese makers made the same magnificent varnish as the great painters of the fifteenth, sixteenth, and seventeenth centuries, and out of the same materials. It was not worth anybody's while to write down a scientific analysis of its composition, and by the time that the introduction of quick-drying varnishes, made of raw spirit and hard gums (shellac was the murderer of the Cremonese varnish) had relegated the tender oil-varnishes of Cremona to oblivion, the composition of the varnish used by Raphael, Amati, Rembrandt, and Stradivarius was forgotten. The world awakened to find that it had suffered the grievous loss of a recipe, once too common to be worth writing down. The *varnish* became panoplied with the dim magnificence

of myth, and gave every ingenious charlatan
the opportunity to exclaim (at decent
intervals) Eureka! With Ruskin one can
fancy that one hears "the chuckle of the
gods in the background."

Charles Reade propounded an ingenious
theory of an under-stain, then a soft oil-
varnish, and, on the top, a brilliant spirit-
varnish. The Messrs Hill equally ingeniously
endeavour to annihilate the theory, but we
do not think they succeed.

But we will summarise our opinion in a
daring proposition. The varnish made and
used to-day by Hill, by Chanot, by Gand, by
Simowtre, and by one or two others, is as fine
as any varnish that the Amatis or Stradivarius
ever made or used. It is *not* the Cremona
varnish. It has no need to be, for, if
anything, it is better.

THE MANNER OF PRESERVING
AND PLAYING THE VIOLIN

CHAT VI.

THE MANNER OF PRESERVING AND PLAYING THE VIOLIN.

IF you want to play the violin well you must love your instrument first. You must reverence it and care for it, and have faith in its powers as though it were a human being, and in addition you must tend it and discipline it as if it were a child. Love your fiddle and it will return love for love; treat it neglectfully and the results will be various and irritating.

For instance, omit to shut your violin away in its snug case, and you will find him husky and shrill when next you meet. Omit to wipe the rosin from the strings, and he will retaliate by sounding scratchy. Omit to clean the neck and finger-board, and he will stick to your hand like a leech. Take your violin to a very hot climate and he will come unstuck; take him to a damp one and he

will be as wheezy as any bronchial patient;
leave him in a draught and he will treat you
to a series of uncalled for harmonics. Hang
him in a museum and his articulation will
grow stiff; let him fall and he cracks or
splits, or his head comes off, and you have to
take him like a lame dog to a vet. to be
bound up.

All these things are liable to happen to
him if he is uncared for, and only the hands
of those who love him can protect his
delicate construction and guard his health.

To accomplish his hygienic treatment you
must first discipline yourself in regular habits;
always wipe your fiddle with a soft silk
handkerchief after playing, gently get the
rosin from the strings and off the belly, also
wipe the finger-board, and immediately put
it away in its case and shut it up.

Nothing spoils a violin so much as allowing
it to lie about exposed to all kinds of
temperatures. When you put it in the case,
really shut the case, and do not put your
violin in carelessly and hurriedly, leaving the
lid half resting on it as one is often tempted
to do. When you have shut it in its case,
find a place to put it where the temperature
is about the same; I mean by this that when

you are at home try and keep your violin always in the same place, and select a corner where the wall is neither hot nor damp, and where there is no draught.

Another very necessary point for the preservation of your fiddle's health is to have a good case to keep it in ; the case should be strongly made of wood, and should be constructed so as to shut closely. If you have a valuable violin an outside cover of mackintosh cloth to strap over is necessary for greater protection from damp.

The next thing you must look after are your strings ; do not leave them on too long or they become dry and hard and will cease to give clear sounds. Of course this remark does not apply to the E string—for this highest and finest of the four strings breaks easily—but only to the thicker ones, the A D and G, which last months. When you buy strings don't go to a piano or music shop for them, but to the best fiddle-maker you can find, for the manufacture of violin strings is just as varied as the manufacture of violins : good, bad, and indifferent. Be specially careful where you purchase them, for a poor string will do much towards spoiling your fiddle's tone. The finest strings

are Italian and are made from the intestines of
lambs in Rome, Naples, Padua and Florence,
some also in Germany and England. Of these
the best are generally considered to be Roman
strings.   They can always be purchased by
post or otherwise at first-rate fiddle-makers
like Hills in London.   Keep your spare
strings in a close-shutting tin box, as they
are very sensitive to heat, damp, and cold ;
also cut off the length you require for
your fiddle and put the rest away in your tin
box.   Don't be disheartened if you find the
best strings do not always sound satisfactory,
for even amongst these you will find that
bête noir of violinists—a false string.   When
this occurs there are but two things to be
done : the first is to try how your string
sounds by turning it upside down on your
fiddle, and if it still sounds badly, the second
thing remains to be done : this constitutes
throwing the string into the fire or out of the
window or into the waste-paper basket. Do it
quietly, I beg of you ! for though there are
few things more irritating than a false string,
still, losing one's temper often makes one
inclined to fling the violin after the string,
and to see your pet Strad flying out of the
window would cause you much grief later.

Don't let other people handle your violin unless they are good amateurs; people who are unaccustomed to a fiddle handle it awkwardly and often give it unmerited bumps. Don't leave it about on chairs where people are liable to sit on it and crush it to pieces. Finally, if after following these foregoing directions your fiddle's tone is unpleasing, take it to a good fiddle-maker and have it thoroughly overhauled.

A Few Hints on Playing.

Among Dr Johnson's many wise sayings few are more erudite than his appreciation of the difficulties of violin playing:

"There is nothing, I think, in which the power of art is shown so much as in playing on the fiddle. In all other things we can do something at first; any man will forge a bar of iron if you give him a hammer, not so well as a smith, but tolerably, and make a box though a clumsy one; but give *him a fiddle and a fiddlestick and he can do nothing.*"

Charles Lamb once startled a select assembly by declaring he would rather see

Judas Iscariot than anyone else in the
world. Lamb was not a fiddler or I am
sure he would have given the preference to
seeing Dr Johnson play the fiddle and
gravely shake his head over its nasty little
ways. Probably Mr Boswell also had a
try and perhaps found out the difficulty of
putting down that tiresome little finger.
But did he divine that there is much of
importance before one ever reaches that
little finger stage? *First* and foremost, there
is the position of the body. Now I never
can understand why people who ordinarily
walk well, stand well, and hold themselves
with upright dignity should suddenly slouch
the moment they place the fiddle under
their chin. This slouch and facial con-
tortions (of which I shall speak later) are
the two greatest faults of the amateur
violinist. Why is this? Why is it necessary
for Apollo and Venus to lose their perfect
symmetry and turn themselves into poor
misshapen hunchbacks because they "saw
the catgut with the horse's tail."

The answer, nine cases out of ten, is bad
teaching! Once start with an *unnatural*
and therefore *wrong* position, and it is
doubtful whether you will ever have the

time or courage to break yourself of this bad habit. When you ride, or drive, or walk, or sing, or dance, you pride yourself on the straight manner you hold yourself: then why not also stand just as proudly and uprightly when you exercise that precious accomplishment—your violin-playing.

The first thing to conquer is to learn to stand with graceful ease; lean a little on the left foot and advance the right—similar to the first position in dancing. Then take your fiddle by the neck and rest it lightly on your *collar bone, not on your shoulder.* Place your chin lightly and easily on the chin rest, but *don't hunch up your shoulder,* or grip your fiddle between chin and shoulder. If you could only see the horrid round back you get when you do this, I am certain you would be disgusted.

Always incline yourself more backward than forward; if you allow yourself to get into the habit of leaning over, you will end by showing only the top of your head to your auditors. This gives an expression-less effect, and makes your neck ache into the bargain.

Standing quite straight with your fiddle lightly poised on your collar bone, twist

your left wrist round to the right, bend
your fingers and place them on the finger-
board as in the accompanying diagram.

Tuck your arm against your side so that
it forms an angle of support for your fiddle,
and *don't allow your thumb to pull backwards towards the scroll.* This is difficult to
prevent at first, but is to be overcome with
patience and determination.

Take your bow in your right hand ; place
the ball of your thumb well on the nut,
allow the other fingers to fall naturally and
gracefully over the stick. Be careful to
place them so that your thumb comes
opposite your middle finger. Raise your
arm naturally, keeping the elbow down, and
bend the wrist gracefuly. Imagine your arm
is a swan's neck and you will get the right
curve. Put your bow on the lowest string,
with the hair slightly turned towards your
face. Draw your arm *away* from you going
down, and *towards* you coming back. Do
this on all the open strings in front of a
looking-glass before you essay to make
notes on the strings with your fingers.

When you have attained some command
over your bow by drawing it twenty times
or so over each string slowly, you can turn to

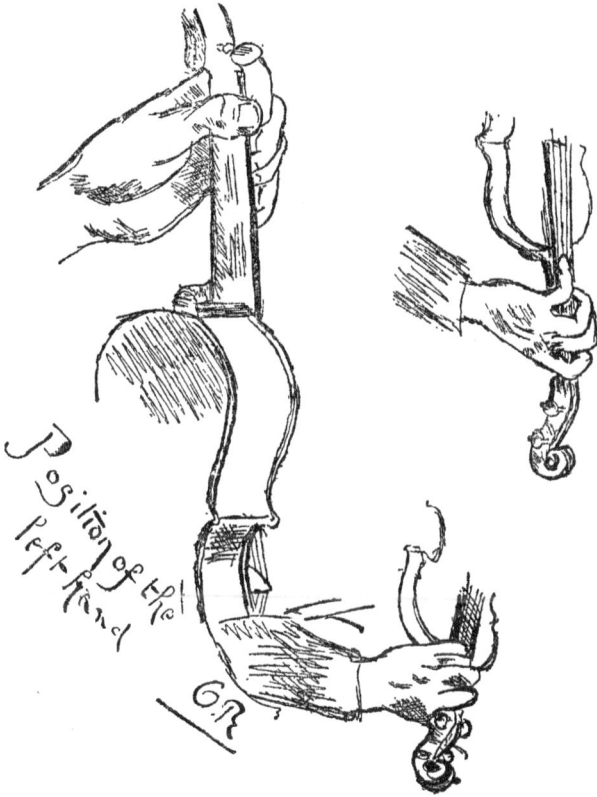

Position of the
Left hand

GR

your instruction book. A good elementary
tutor is H. E. Rayser's Op. 65, but should
you prefer a complete work De Beriot's or
Dancla's *Violin Schools* are gradually pro-
gressive. Go squarely through any one of
these schools and with patience they will
carry you far. *Be careful to play always on
the tips of your fingers*, and place them firmly
on the strings; and, above all, guard against
any grotesqueness of manner and expression.
A bad position of the body and distorted
features utterly spoil an otherwise meritorious
performance.

Few amateurs realise the importance of
appropriateness of expression. The majority
appear to be either on the verge of tears
or as though they had pickles in their
mouths; some assume a martial air, while
others smile so foolishly that one trembles
for their reason. Why not think of the
interpretation of the music you are playing,
and the expression of your face will in-
voluntarily change according to the mood
of the composer?

If Henry Irving or Ellen Terry acted
tragic parts with a comedy smile or *vice versâ*
you would be the first to say how grotesque!
If Mdme. Patti sang "Comin' thro' the Rye"

with a heavy frown, Paderewski interpreted
a wild Liszt Fantasia with an expressionless
face, or Sarasate gnashed his teeth while playing a graceful "Spanish Dance," you would
say, "How incongruous!" Why? Because
their individual expression would spoil their
art, just as a beautiful painted landscape
would be completely marred by the introduction of an unsuitable subject in the fore-
ground.

Breathe the music from your face; stand
erect, and you will have accomplished much,
for you will appear genial even during the
operation of playing.

.   .   .   .

Written instructions on violin-playing are
only a slight assistance to the earnest self-
taught student who welcomes them on the
system of "half a loaf being better than
none." Self education is, of course, most
meritorious, and, in some branches of
learning, successfully accomplished, but in
the case of playing on the tantalising little
wooden box, quite impossible.

You must have a teacher. You must be
personally shown the thousand and one
little subtleties, indescribable by means of
the pen; you must be watched out of your

faults, and you must be guided in your choice of music, so that your progress is gradual.

The great difficulty in these days when all men fiddle a bit is to find a thoroughly good instructor. People either choose the first master (with a foreign name) who comes to hand, or rush off to some popular star, ignoring the fact that a great executant is rarely a great teacher. Nine cases out of ten, the strain of concert work precludes a popular *virtuoso* from giving anything but a few finishing lessons. When you have conquered detail, and understand your technique thoroughly, go to your great artist, and drink in the grandeur of his perfection, but for early instruction, choose in preference one of his pupils, or the pupil of some great academy, who is esteemed more for his teaching powers, than his executive gifts.

So much disheartenment is caused by bad instruction in the early stages of learning, that the urgency of being well taught in the beginning cannot be too much insisted on.

Though it is not easy for the uninitiated to choose a master, the difficulty of finding

a fiddle worth the price we pay for it, is far
harder.   Where shall we buy it?

> "this small sweet thing.
> Devised in love and fashioned cunningly
> Of wood and strings."

Shall we go to the toy shop over the way,
and gaze at it lying there, truly small,
doubtfully sweet, made of highly - coloured
splintering wood, and temptingly offered for
1s.?   Shall   we   with   palpitating   heart
enter   the   local   music   shop,   and   handle
a   bright   shining   specimen,   price   £1?
Shall we glance cautiously round the old
curiosity   shop   where   (though   we   know
nothing about it) we erroneously think we
may   discover   a   grand   old   Cremona   for
10s.?   Or   shall   we   go   to   the   fountain
head ; to Mirecourt in France, or Mittenwald
in Germany, and see the "small sweet thing,"
grossly fashioned in thousands, by machinery?
If we can only afford a moderate sum, we
can here dispense it in a counterfeit Cremona
duely labled and bearing that burnt representation of age which would never deceive
an expert.

   But if our golden ducats are as plentiful
as the fowls of the air, then must we throw

aside all thoughts of a solo tour of inspection, and seek the sheltering advice of the calm connoisseur.   His assistance and protection are most necessary, for, as the Rev. H. R. Haweis has said: "There are three things in this world about which, otherwise respectable people seem to have no conscience— horses, umbrellas, and last, but not least, fiddles.   The fact is, the public in general knows nothing about fiddles, and so is very easily gulled."   Don't trust to your own powers to buy a high-priced fiddle : get some one of experience to help you ; go to one of the leading fiddle-makers, like Hill or Hart in London, Vuillaume, Gand and Bernadel or Chanot in Paris, Gemünder, in New York, be well advised about your choice, and get a guarantee with your purchase.   In this way you will be pretty certain to obtain the worth of your money.

In conclusion, remember that the most exquisitely contrived fiddle in the world may be turned into an instrument of torture by unskilful hands.

"The soul of music slumbers in the shell,
    Till wakened and kindled by the master's spell."

It is you who have the power to rouse

this hidden soul, and bid it, with a magic touch, soar far beyond the skies, leaving the stars far behind. See that you value your prlvilege, and reverently use it; for, as Plato has truly said: "Music is a moral law. It gives a soul to the universe, wings to the mind, flight to the imagination, a charm to sadness, gaiety and life in everything. It is the essence of order and leads to all that is good, just and beautiful, of which it is the invisible, but nevertheless dazzling, passionate and eternal form."

APPENDIX

APPENDIX.

Biographic Sketches: Nicolo Paganini.

THE power of natural genius, in bursting
forth under every species of disadvantage and
impediment, has been seldom so triumphantly
manifested as in the life of Paganini, the
musician. To excel in music as a science,
does not require, by any means, a high order
of intellect, neither does it demand that
extraordinary cultivation by art necessary
in the pursuit of the other sciences; but to
be perfect in its theory and practice, much
intuitive ability, and a happy expertness,
are requisite; for without these, the aspirant
will, in general, only reach a respectable
mediocrity, hardly worthy of being attained.
In the life of the renowned personage now
to be noticed it will be seen that genius was
born with him, and soon made itself known.

Nicolo Paganini was born at Genoa in
February, 1784; it is not mentioned what his
father's profession was, if indeed he had any;

and all we are told is, that his chief pursuit was to improve his circumstances, which were not the best in the world, by speculating in the lottery ; so that when his little son, Nicolo, began, at an unusually early age, to give strong indications of musical talent, it seemed as if the wheel of fortune had at last been propitious, and he accordingly lost no time in setting to work to make the most of his prize.   Having some skill on the violin himself, he resolved to teach him that instrument, and, as soon as he could hold it, put one into his hands, and made him sit beside him from morning till night to practice it. The incessant drudgery which he compelled him to undergo, and the occasional starvation to which he subjected him, seriously impaired his health, and, as Paganini himself asserts, laid the foundation of that valetudinarian state which has ever since been his portion, and which his pale sickly countenance and his sunk and exhausted frame so strongly attest.   As his enthusiasm was such as to require no artificial stimulus, this severe system could only have been a piece of cool and wanton barbarity.

In his eighth year, under the superintendence of his father, he had written a sonata, which, however, along with many other juvenile productions, he lately destroyed ; and, as he played about three times a week in the churches and at private musical parties, upon a fiddle nearly a large as himself, he soon began to make himself known among his townsmen. At this time he received much benefit from one Francesco Gnecco, who died in 1811, and whom he always speaks highly of.

In his ninth year, being applied to by a travelling singer to join him in a concert, he made his first public appearance in the great theatre at Genoa, and played the French air, "La Carmagnole," with his own variations, with great applause.

His father now resolved to place him under the tuition of the well-known composer, Rolla, and for that purpose took him along with him to Parma. The particulars of their interview afford a striking proof of the proficiency which he had by this time acquired. As Rolla happened to be ill and lying in bed, the party were shown into the antechamber, when, observing upon the table one of the composer's newest concertos, the father beckoned to his son to take up his violin and play it, which he did at sight, in such a way that the sick man immediately started up, demanded who it was, and could scarcely be prevailed upon to believe that the sounds had proceeded from a little boy, and his intended pupil; but, as soon as he had satisfied himself that that was really the case, he declined to receive him—"For God's sake," said he, "go to Paer; your time would be lost with me; I can do nothing for you."

To Paer accordingly they went, who received him kindly, and referred him to his own teacher, the old and experienced

"Maestro di Capella" Girettti, from Naples, who gave him instructions for six months, three times a week in counterpoint. During this period he wrote twenty-four fugues for four hands, with pen, ink, and paper alone, and without an instrument, which his master did not allow him, and assisted by his own inclination, made rapid progress. The great Paer also took much interest in him, giving him compositions to work out, which he himself revised, an interest for which Paganini ever afterwards showed himself deeply grateful.

The time was now come when Nicolo was destined, like other youthful prodigies, to be hawked about the country, to fill the pockets of his mercenary father, who managed to speculate upon him with considerable success in Milan, Bologna, Florence, Pisa, Leghorn, and most of the upper and central towns of Italy, where his concerts were always well attended. Young Paganini liked these excursions well enough; but, being now about fifteen years of age, he began to be of opinion that they would be still more agreeable if he could only contrive to get rid of the old gentleman, whose spare diet and severe discipline had now become more irksome to him than ever. To accomplish this desirable object an opportunity soon offered. It was the custom of Lucca, at the feast of Saint Martin, to hold a great musical festival to which strangers were invited from all quarters, and numerous travellers resorted

of their own accord; and as the occasion
drew near, Nicolo begged hard to be allowed
to go there in company with his elder brother;
and, after much entreaty succeeded in obtaining permission. He made his appearance as
a solo player, and succeeded so well, that he
resolved now to commence vagabondising
on his own account—a sort of life to which
he soon became so partial that, notwithstanding many handsome offers which he
occasionally received to establish himself
in several places as a concerto player, or
director of the orchestra, he never could be
persuaded to settle anywhere. At a later
period, however, he lived for some time at
the Court of Lucca; but soon found it more
pleasant and profitable to resume his itinerant
habits. He visited all parts of Italy, but
usually made Genoa his headquarters, where,
however, he preferred to play the part of the
dilettante to that of the *virtuoso*, and performed in private circles without giving public
concerts.

It was not long before he had amassed
about 20,000 francs, part of which he proposed to devote to the maintenance of his
parents. His father, however, was not to
be put off with a few thousands, but insisted
upon the whole. Paganini then offered him
the interest of the capital, but Signor Antonio
very coolly threatened him with instant death,
unless he agreed to consign the whole of
the principal in his behalf; and in order
to avert serious consequences, and to procure

peace, he gave up the greater part of it.

Those who know anything of the gay, romantic sort of life which artists in Italy, particularly those connected with the all-engrossing object of music, usually lead, the diversified society in which they mingle, and the incident and adventure which they meet with, will not wonder that Paganini should have felt inclined to pass his days there, among his own countrymen, who felt and appreciated his talent, received him upon all occasions with the most enthusiastic applause, and showered down upon him all the gold they could afford, besides flowers, garlands, and sonnets, in abundance. He loved the manners and customs of his country, its beautiful scenery, its climate; but their kindred souls were still more congenial to his heart. He was their idol; wherever he went his fame preceded his approach, and the multitudes poured in to hear him in streams as if he had been a worker of miracles. Having music at their command at all hours of the day, there is no country where concerts are worse attended than in Italy, and yet those which he gave never failed. People seemed never to be satiated with the delight of hearing him; and at Milan he gave, with the most brilliant success, no fewer than nineteen concerts rapidly succeeding each other. The only place in the whole of his peregrinations where he was unsuccessful was at Palermo in Sicily. At Rome, Naples, and Florence, he was eminently triumphant, and at the former of these places, His Holiness the Pope was pleased to confer upon him the Order of the Speron d'Oro.

It was early in 1828 when Paganini arrived at Vienna, where he gave a great many concerts with a success equal, if not superior, to any which had hitherto attended his exertions. His performance excited the admiration and astonishment of all the most distinguished professors and connoisseurs of this critical city. With any of the former all idea of competition was hopeless; and their great violinist, Mayseder, as soon as he had heard him, with an ingenuousness which did him honour, as we ourselves have reason to know, wrote to a friend in London, that he might now lock up his violin whenever he liked.

In estimating the labour which it must have cost a performer like Paganini to have arrived at such transcendent excellence, people are often apt to err in their calculations as to the actual extent of time and practice which has been devoted to its acquisition. That the perfect knowledge of the *mechanique* of the instrument which his performance exhibits, and his almost incredible skill and dexterity in its management, must necessarily have been the result of severe discipline, is beyond all question; but more, much more, in every case of this kind, is to be ascribed to the system upon which that discipline has proceeded, and to the genius and enthusiasm of the artist. The miraculous powers of Paganini, in the opinion of his auditors, were not to be accounted for in the ordinary way. To them it was plain that they must have sprung from a life of a much more settled and secluded cast, than that of an itinerant Italian musical professor. It was equally clear, from his wild, haggard and mysterious looks, that he was no ordinary personage, and had seen no common vicissitudes. The vaults of a dungeon accordingly were the local habitation which public rumour, in its love of the marvellous, seemed unanimously to assign to him, as the only place where " the mighty magic" of his bow could possibly have been acquired.

Then, as to the delinquency which led to his incarceration, there were various accounts. Some imputed it to his having been a captain of banditti; others, only a carbonaro; some to his having killed a man in a duel: but the more current and generally received story was, that he had stabbed or poisoned his wife, or, as some said, his mistress; although, as fame had ascribed to him no fewer than four mistresses, it was never very clearly made out which of his seraglio it was who had fallen the victim of his vengeance. The story not improbably might have arisen from his having been confounded with a contemporary violin player, of the name of Duranowski, a Pole, to whom in person he bore some resemblance, and who, for some offence or other, having been imprisoned at Milan, during the leisure which his captivity afforded had contrived greatly to improve himself in his art; and when once it was embodied into shape, the fiction naturally enough might have obtained the more evidence, from the fact that two of his most distinguished predecessors, Tartini and Lolly, had attained to the great mastery which they possessed over their instrument during a period of solitude—the one within the walls of a cloister—the other in the privacy and retirement of a remote country village; at all events, the rumours were universally circulated and believed, and the innocent and much injured Paganini had for many years unconsciously stood forth in the eyes of the world as a violator of the laws, and even a convicted murderer. He seems never to have been made fully aware of the formidable position in which he stood until he had reached Vienna, when the *Theatrical Gazette*, in reviewing his first concert, dropped some pretty broad hints as to the rumoured misdeeds of his earlier life. Whereupon he resolved at once publicly to proclaim his innocence, and to put down the calumny; for which purpose, on the 10th April 1828, there was inserted in the leading Vienna journals, a manifesto, in Italian as well as German, subscribed by him, declaring that all these widely circulated rumours were false; that at no time, and under no govern-

ment whatever, had he ever offended against
the laws, or been put under coercion ; and
that he had always demeaned himself as
became a peaceable and inoffensive member
of society ; for the truth of which he referred
to the magistrates of the different states,
under whose protection he had till then
lived in the public exercise of his profession.
No one dared to invalidate the truth of
this appeal.

His command of the back string of the
instrument has always been an especial
theme of wonder and admiration, and, in
the opinion of some, could only be accounted
for by resorting to the theory of the dungeon
and the supposition that his other strings
being worn out, and not having it in his
power to supply their places, he had been
forced from necessity to take refuge in the
string in question ; a notion very like that
of a person who would assert, that for an
opera dancer to learn to stand on one leg ;
the true way would be—to have only one
leg to stand upon. We shall give Paganini's
explanation of this mystery in his own
words.

" At Lucca, I had always to direct the
opera when the reigning family visited the
theatre ; I played three times a week at the
Court, and every fortnight superintended the
arrangement of a grand concert for the Court-
parties, which, however, the reigning princess,
Elisa Bacciochi, Princess of Lucca and
Piombino, Napoleon's favourite sister, was

not always present at, or did not hear to the
close, as the harmonic tones of my violin
were apt to grate her nerves, but there never
failed to be present another much esteemed
lady, who, while I had long admired her,
bore (at least so I imagined) a reciprocal
feeling towards me. Our passion gradually
increased, and as it was necessary to keep it
concealed, the footing on which we stood
with each other became in consequence the
more interesting. One day I promised to
surprise her with a musical *jeu d'esprit* which
should have a reference to our mutual attach-
ment.   I accordingly announced for performance a comic novelty, to which I gave
the name of 'Love Scene.'   All were
curiously impatient to know what this should
turn out to be, when I at last appeared with
my violin, from which I had taken off the two
middle strings, leaving only the E and G
string. By the first of these I proposed to
represent the lady, by the other the
gentleman ; and I proceeded to play a sort of
dialogue, in which I attempted to delineate
the capricious quarrel and reconciliations of
lovers ; at one time scolding each other, at
another sighing and making tender advances,
renewing their professions of love and esteem,
and finally winding up the scene in the
utmost good humour and delight. Having
at last brought them into a state of the most
perfect harmony, the united pair lead off a
pas de deux, concluding with a brilliant finale.
This musical scene went off with much

N

éclat. The lady, who understood the whole
perfectly, rewarded me with her gracious
looks, the princess was all kindness, over-
whelmed me with applause, and, after com-
plimenting me upon what I had been able
to effect upon the two strings, expressed
a wish to hear what I could execute
upon one string.   I immediately assented ;
the idea caught my fancy; and as the
Emperor's birthday took place a few weeks
afterwards, I composed my sonata, 'Napoleon'
for the G string, and performed it upon
that day before the Court with so much
approbation, that a cantata of Cimarosa,
following immediately after it upon the same
evening, was completely extinguished, and
produced no effect whatever. This is the
first and true cause of my partiality for the G
string, and as they were always desiring to
hear more of it, one day taught another, until
at last my proficiency in this department was
completely established."

No one has been more cruelly mis-
represented than the subject of this notice.
In reality a person of the gentlest and most
inoffensive habits, he is anything rather than
the desperate ruffian he has been described.
In his dmeanour he is modest and unassum-
ing to a fault. Like most artists, ardent and
enthusiastic in his temperament, and in his
actions very much a creature of impulse, he is
full of all that simplicity which we almost
invariably find associated with true genius.
He has an only son, a very precocious child,

who already indicates strong signs of musical talent. Being of a delicate frame of health, Paganini never can bear to trust him out of his sight. "If I were to lose him," says he, "I would be lost myself; it is quite impossible that I can ever separate myself from him, when I awake in the night, he is my first thought." Accordingly, ever since he parted from his mother, he has himself enacted the part of a child's nurse. Nor in his filial duties is he more remiss than in the parental. The wealth which he has amassed has been partly applied to provide for the comforts of an aged mother, and not unfrequently dispensed in acts of bounty towards his more necessitous relations and friends.

The above life of Paganini we have condensed from an able account of him, which appeared upwards of a twelvemonth ago in an extremely useful and meritorious publication, devoted to continental literature, under the title of the *Foreign Quarterly Review*. Since then, the genius of the violin, as he may be called, has paid a professional visit to Great Britain and Ireland, in which countries he is understood to have reaped very large sums. Ultimately, we believe, he intends to retire to the Continent, to enjoy his gains in Tuscany, the climate of which he prefers to all others. *Chamber's Edinburgh Journal*, 20th October 1832.

Paganini.

The sensation which this violinist has caused among all classes in London is so universal and extraordinary that we really feel embarrassed in taking up the pen on the present occasion. The daily and weekly journals have been full of Paganani this fortnight and more—Paganini has been the all-absorbing topic of conversation in every circle, from the *salon* to the tap-room, and the speculations upon Reform in the national representation yielded, for a time, to the universal clamour for reform in the prices of admission at which the most opulent capital of the universe was to enjoy the magic of a solitary fiddle.

. . . .

In the spring of the present year he reluctantly quitted a country, the cordiality and musical susceptibilities of whose inhabitants had made him feel at home wherever he set his foot, and arrived at Paris, undecided whether ultimately he would venture across the Channel to satisfy the anxious longings of the British public. In Paris, where he sojourned about six weeks, the astonishment which his performances created was as great and universal as it had been at Vienna, Dresden, and Berlin ; and the concerts, the admission to which was doubled, as it had been in all those cities, are stated to have yielded a net gain of about £5,000.

The prospect of a lucrative speculation so near at hand was not neglected by the manager of the King's Theatre in London. Mr Laporte succeeded in conquering Signor Paganini's hesitation to appear among us, by holding out confident expectations of a golden harvest. Mr Laporte was to give the King's Theatre for the performance of eight concerts, terminating on the 20th of June; he was also to furnish singers and orchestra; the prices were to be doubled, and one-third of the gross receipts, with some incidental advantages, in disposing of a few boxes and admissions, was to be Mr Laporte's share of the venture.

These terms being mutually agreed upon Signor Paganini, immediately on his arrival, announced his intention to give a grand miscellaneous concert on the 21st of May, upon the following terms of admission:— *Boxes*, Pit tier, eight guineas; ground tier, ten guineas; one pair, nine guineas; two pair, six guineas; three pair, four guineas. *Stalls*, two guineas; *Orchestra*, one and a half guineas; *Pit*, one guinea; *Gallery*, half-a-guinea.

These prices were universally considered as extravagant, and loudly protested against by the editors of the leading daily papers, and by numerous letters from their correspondents, which led to an animated contest. On the one hand, it was contended that Signor Paganini had doubled the usual prices of admission wherever he played, in

Germany as well as in France; while the
opponents showed, by simple calculation,
that a full house on the terms demanded
would produce between three and four
thousand pounds every night—*i.e.*, for about
one hour's play of the *virtuoso* a sum
tantamount to an independent fortune in
Italy! and as to the plea of Signor Paganini
having doubled his prices on the Continent,
it was justly observed, that if he had fixed
upon Drury Lane or Covent Garden for
the display of his talent, no reasonable
objection could have been made to his
doubling the usual prices of admission at
those theatres; but the case was altered by
his selecting the Opera House, one of the
largest theatres in Europe, in which the
ordinary prices of admission were already
three times as much as those of our other
national theatres.

Without expatiating farther on the fluc-
tuating features of this contest, which at
one time threatened to terminate in the
departure of the artist without so much as
unpacking his instrument, it may be sufficient
to add, that his better judgment, as well as
a sense for his real interest, induced him to
yield to the voice of the public and to the
advice of judicious and sincere friends, and
to announce definitely his first concert for
Friday, the 3rd of June, at the prices usually
paid for admission to the Italian Opera at
the King's Theatre—a determination which,
as the result has proved, he will have no

reason to regret. There can be no question but that his receipts at double prices, even without the interference of the Press, would have fallen far short of the amount which the ordinary terms of admission have already yielded, and are likely to produce hereafter. *New Monthly Magazine*, 31st July 1831.

Paganini.

The near approach of the appearance of this extraordinary performer before the London public, may render the following extracts from a description of him in *Le Globe* interesting to our readers:

" Paganini and his violin enter. A universal clapping welcomes his appearance on the stage. He advances several paces with embarrassment, and bows; and the applause recommences. He proceeds with a gait still more and more awkward, and is again applauded. He bows repeatedly, and endeavours to throw into his countenance a smile of acknowledgment, which is soon, however, replaced by an icy coldness of expression.

" He stops, and in a position in which he seems, if possible, still more constrained than during his walk and his salutations. He seizes his violin, places it between his chin and his breast, and casts on it a proud look, at once piercing and sweet. He stands thus for several seconds, leaving the public

time to observe and examine his strange
originality; to gaze with curiosity at his
lank body, his long arms and fingers, his
chestnut - coloured hair flowing over his
shoulders, the illness and suffering imprinted
on his whole person, his sunken mouth, his
long hawk-nose, his pale and hollow cheeks,
his large, fine, and open forehead, which
Dr Gall would love to contemplate, and
under that forehead eyes, hidden as if in
shade, but every instant darting forth
lightning.

"Suddenly, his looks descend from his
violin to the orchestra. He gives the signal,
and, abruptly raising his right hand in the
air, lets his bow fall upon his violin. You
expect that all the strings are about to be
broken. Nothing of the sort. You are
surprised by the lightest, the most delicate,
the finest of sounds. For several instants
he continues to play with your anticipations,
and to provoke you. All the caprices which
occur to him are employed to rouse you
from the indifference which he supposes you
to feel. He runs, he leaps from tones to
tones, from octaves to octaves, passes with
incredible swiftness and precision the wildest
distances; ascends and descends natural and
chromatic gamuts; produces everywhere
harmonic chords; draws forth the most
extraordinary sounds of which the violin is
capable; makes it speak, sing, complain;
now there is a murmuring of waves, now

a breeze of wind, now a chirping of birds; in short, an incoherent *charivari*.

"This great artist has, however, other resources than such fantasies for the captivation of the public. To this musical phantasmagoria presently succeeds a broad, grand, and harmonious simplicity. Pure, sweet, brilliant, tuneful chords flow from his bow; sounds which seem to proceed from the heart, and which plunge you into a state of delicious feeling. Then comes a vague sighing of melancholy and self-abandonment. While you are sympathising with the touching and melodious performer, a sudden access of violent grief, a sort of shuddering and rage, appears to seize him; and cries which penetrate the depths of the soul alarm and freeze you, and make you tremble for the unfortunate being whom you see and hear!"

Such is a Parisian picture of this extraordinary performer, respecting whom we observe a great discord has been produced in the newspapers, which is likely at least to postpone the period of his appearing before an English audience. We will not enter into the dispute, whether the doubling of the Opera prices was extravagant or justifiable (prices have been doubled in every place where he has played), but in justice to Mr Laporte, we wish to bear testimony to his constant and liberal efforts to please the public in the very difficult situation he occupies. If the intended charge on this

occasion was too high, nobody needed to pay it unless they liked—the offence would have brought its own punishment. And really we do not know a trader who happens to import a rare or superior article of commerce, and who, out of pure generosity, chooses to sell it at the cost of a less valuable or attractive commodity. Altogether, how-ever, as the King's Theatre prices are con-siderable, we think it would have been wiser in M. Paganini to content himself with them.—
The Literay Gazette and *Journal of the Belles Letters*, 21st May, 1831.

Paganini.

The *début* of this extraordinary man was all that admiration and enthusiasm could anticipate. His performances are not merely wonderful—they are beyond measure delight-ful. It is not simply such command of an instrument as never was witnessed before—it is the production of music which may literally be said to ravish the sense. Paganini himself seems as if he were an exquisite incar-nation of composition—harmony embodied in a human frame. No description can convey an idea of his powers ; and every journal has been so filled with remarks, that were we competent to do justice to his genius, we should abstain from a task which must of necessity involve so much of repetition. Our recommendation to every one is—make a point of hearing him ; it will be a gratification beyond belief, and to miss it, a very severe regret. Old Cramer, it is said, exclaimed, he was glad he was not a fiddler, implying that the impossibility of attaining such excellence would have broken his heart, and I. Cooke, declares that Paganini is equal to any four he ever saw. Such are the flattering testimonies of his brethren. We may notice that his hand, and especially his thumb, which is of uncommon length, give him the unexampled facilities which he possesses over his violin.— The *Literary Gazette* and *Journal of the Belles Letters*, 11th *June* 1831.

Paganini !!
His début *at the Opera-House last night.*

At length all differences have been arranged, and the mighty wonder has come forth—a very Zamiel in appearance, and certainly a very devil in performance! He is, beyond rivalry, the bow-ideal of fiddling facility! He possesses a demon-like influence over his instrument, and makes it utter sounds almost superhuman. In his concerto of three movements, a cadenza at the end of the allegro literally appalled us—this, by the way, is the truest bit of violin-playing in his whole performance. His " Sonata Militaire," on the subject of Mozart's *Non piu andria*, was played with astonishing precision and expression, although circumscribed to the limits of the 4th string, which the Signor invests with all the powers of the other three.

His mixture of *pizzicato* with his bowing is quite his own, and is likely ever to remain so. The arrival of this magician is quite enough to make the greater part of the fiddling tribe commit suicide. Never was there a more rapturous reception; it was a most musical house, and enthusiasm was the order of the night. We shall notice at more detail the peculiarities of this extraordinary man's performance next week; want of space and time prevents us from more than the present. —*The Athenæum, 4th June* 1831.

Paganini.

" Music ! oh, how faint, how weak,
Language fades before thy spell ! "
—MOORE.

In our last, and of necessity hurried notice, we could only speak of this extraordinary man in general terms of delight and admiration; and now, with even some days of cool reflection to our aid, we feel that we have not the *ingenium par materiæ* properly to describe him. He stands alone; and it is quite as desponding a task to explain his peculiarities of superiorship to other violinists, as it would be to picture the grandeur of the Falls of Niagara to one whose notions of the "thunder of the waters" never extended beyond the tide-fall of the Thames at old London Bridge. Really, those who have not heard him, and more particularly those who are unacquainted with the practical difficulties he has conquered, cannot form any adequate notion of his wonderful and entrancing power. He strings his violin very thinly; nevertheless, there is a roundness and silkiness of tone which is at once delightful and astonishing. Sorrow is the characteristic of his style and music; and although some French author has said that *La melancolie est toujours friande*, it certainly never was half so delicious as it appears in this strange being's performance. He literally imparts an animal sensibility to his instrument, and at moments makes it wail and moan with all the truth and expression of conscious physical suffering. We could not refrain from personifying, in fact thinking that the poor violin was a transformed victim in a demon's hands, uttering the anguished complaints of his inflicted torture. In moments less *appassionati*, it "discoursed most eloquent" tenderness and simple sweetness. A fanciful writer has observed, that the cause of the melancholy which prevails in the Irish melodies is that the harps, whence they have had their origin, were generally made of yew-tree; we should like to know of what wood Paganini's violin is composed. A punning friend of ours at our elbow says it must be *Satan*-wood. Abominable!

Paganini has been accused by some persons of charlatanism; and all because he plays, or rather *fingers*, in one key while the orchestra accompanies him in another. Why, this trick, if trick it be, is as old as Corelli himself, and is as legitimate a mode of producing effect as any good score writer's using a B flat clarionet in the key of E three flats. This is some of the nonsense—criticism which we every day meet with, and which is so very disgusting from its flippant affectation of knowledge. But *charlatanism* is the term bestowed upon everybody who commands the notice of the world by extraordinary means or intelligence. For our parts, we see no trickery in Ducrou's horse-riding, or Michael Boai's chin-chopping —each is perfection *sui generis*; and as to Paganini, the sooner our violinists learn some of *his tricks* the better—for then they will play in time and tune—with expression and power!

We are slow to "swallow mountains," and therefore did not believe all we heard touching the Signor before his arrival. Nay, last year we ventured to back De Beriot against him; we here retract. De Beriot is a sweet, chaste player—but Paganini is a solitary man in his art! There is a relation between an unit and a million—*none between him and his fellow-men.*

One thing more we wish to remark. He plays without a reading-desk or book-stand; this gives an air of improvising to his performance, which we hope to see imitated, if any one be found hardy enough to undertake a violin solo for the next seven years. We shall notice his *appearance on Monday next at length.—The Athenæum*, 11th June 1831.

Paganini.

This musical wonder continues to excite the admiration and curiosity of the public in an extraordinary degree, and is likely to reap the richest harvest of any musical performer known to fame. He has been engaged by Sir George Smart at the Coronation, for which he is to receive 1,000 guineas. The proprietors of Vauxhall Gardens offered him £1,000 for three nights; the offer was refused, and when desired to name his terms, his demand was £5,000 for twelve nights. He is engaged to perform at Liverpool next week, on his way to Ireland; after the Dublin Musical Festival, he will proceed to Cork and Belfast, and from thence to Scotland. His visit to Edinburgh will take place early in October. It is anticipated that the *bowing* of this distinguished foreigner will create a greater sensation in the neighbourhood of Holyrood than has been excited by any disciple of Orpheus since the days of David Rizzio.— *The Constitution or Cork Advertiser*, 25th August, 1831.

PAGANINI.

Of all the beasts which Nature made,
  With just no other view
Than to surprise our mortal eyes
  And show what she could do;
Of monsters in the air or deep,
  Four-footed, furr'd, or finny,
There's none to be compared at all
  To Signor Paganini.

With flowing hair, and forehead pale,
    And eyes of earnest fire,
He's just what Dr Rice would call
    A musical Messiah.
The man that mocks the thrushes, or
    The man that chops his chin, he
Is nothing at all, believe me—no—
    To Signor Paganini.

An air with variations,
    That run up all the score ;
He'll play as well on one string
    As some folks can on four.
A violin's but a fiddle,
    And yet I'll bet a guinea,
A violin turns to what you please,
    In the hands of Paganini.

Each instrument, by turns, it is,
    That sounds in peace or war ;
Now the Apollonican,
    And now the light guitar—
And now it is a little bird,
    That sits up in a tree ;
That sits and sings, 'til another begins,
    And sings as well as he.

All sounds which earthly passion breathes
    With fingers long and limber,
The Signor can elicit from
    This most harmonious timber ;
What does Dr Matthews say?
    Is it not surprising
To hear a little bit of wood
    Mono-poly-logue-ising?

Sometimes it is a beggar woman,
    With an infant at her breast,
With 'plaining moan, and pleading tone,
    Most piteously exprest.

Sometimes a little fretful child
   That roars with desperation,
While Paganini belabours him
   With a right good flagellation.

Sometimes bow and viol struck
   Like flint and steel together,
Give sparkles of sweet sound that fall
   Like stars in frosty weather;
Now lightly glancing, one by one,
   They momently shine and die,
And now in a show'ring profusion of sparks,
   Rocket-like, fall from high.

Sometimes the note breaks forth so large,
   You'd rather not be near it ;
Sometimes so very small and thin,
   You wonder you can hear it :
Suddenly comes a hubbub wild
   Of inarticulate words ;
Is this the House of Commons,
   Or is it the House of Lords?

Last, 'tis some fair cantatrice,
   Whom he holds in his arms,
Gazing most enrapturedly,
   And wildly on her charms ;
" Be mine, sweet maid," the fiddler cries,
   " My life, my love, my hinney ! "
" Not I, you brute ! " the nymph replies,
   " Sweet, do ! " says Paganini.

P. W.

Paganini is, without question, the great musical genius of the age. If report be true however, he does not entertain that contempt for filthy lucre which generally accompanies gifted minds. Various ludicrous stories are circulating in the *coulisses* as to his economics. His concert on Thursday brought together a concourse not often witnessed within the

O

walls of the Opera House. It would have
required an hydraulic press to squeeze
another into the pit. Old Elwes himself
would have been satisfied with the proceeds ;
the Italian, however, grumbled. On someone
congratulating him upon the fulness of the
house, he complained, with a shrug, "that it
would cost him three clean shirts." On his
arrival in England, either the *manx de mir*, or
the air of London, had somewhat indisposed
the musician. He was ordered to take
certain draughts during the night ; and it was
suggested to him that he should burn a
rushlight. On enquiring, however, the price
of that luminary of the night, he swore by the
body of Bacchus (corpo di Bacco) that he
would wait till the daylight broke. We know
not if these *ana* be true, but the invention of
them would testify that they are not
improbable.—*The Examiner*, 26th July 1831.

Paganini Anecdotes.

(Various writers in their accounts of
Paganini have asserted that this great artist
had received a brilliant education, and that he
spoke and wrote all the modern languages,
with the greatest facility. These statements
are erroneous. Paganini neither spoke nor
wrote any language excepting Italian.
Whenever he received persons whose visits
were not actuated by speculative motives, he
would at times abandon himself to the most

extravagant gaiety—his language rolled on
with surprising volubility, and he took a
delight, during such periods, in relating without reserve, and accompanied with fits of
hearty laughter, a variety of singular anecdotes concerning himself. The following
adventure, as coming direct from the lips of
the *maestro*, bears its own peculiar stamp.)

The Cabriolet, related by Paganini.

" One evening," said he, " I found myself in
the streets of Vienna, when the thunder was
growling in the heavens, and the rain dashing
heavily against the windows of the surrounding houses. I had left my hotel, and
was strolling along, without any object in view,
occupied, by way of *distraction*, in examining
the fine square heads of Austrian folk as they
passed. The storm suddenly overtook me in
one of the suburbs. I was alone, which I
seldom am, and before I could reach my home
I had at least half a league to walk. My
only alternative was to stop a coach. I
successively hailed three 'gondolas,' but the
drivers, not understanding the language in
which I addressed them, refused to draw up,
and continued their way. A fourth came by
—the rain fell in torrents, and the storm was
at its height. This time, fortunately, the
driver understood me ; he was an Italian, a
true Italian. Ere entering his vehicle, I was
anxious to fix the fare, and on my putting
the question to him of—

" ' How much do you ask to drive me home
to my hotel ? he replied :

" 'Five florins, the price of admission to
Paganini's concerto.'

" ' Rogue, that you are,' cried I, ' how dare
you ask five florins for so short a lift ?
Paganini plays upon one string, but you, can
you drive your cab upon one wheel ? '

" ' Ah, sir ! ' returned the man, ' it is not so
difficult as people pretend to play upon one
string. I am a musician, and I have this day
doubled my fares to enable me to go and hear
Paganini.'

" I gave over bargaining : the man was
conscientious in his demand. In less than
ten minutes' ride we pulled up at the door of
my house. I took five florins out of my
purse, and a ticket from my pocket-book.'

" ' Here, take your fare ! ' said I to the man,
' and here is a ticket for Paganini's concert ;
he gives one to-morrow in the Philharmonic
Rooms.'

" The following evening, at eight o'clock,
the crowd thronged the approaches of the hall
where I was to be heard. I had only just
arrived, when one of the stewards took me
aside and informed me that there was a man
in a jacket, and otherwise shabbily dressed,
at the door, who was endeavouring to force
his way into the Assembly. I followed, and
recognised my driver of the previous evening
who, asserting the right of admission I had
given him, was seeking to introduce himself,

and vociferating that admittance could not
justly be denied him.

"I immediately changed the veto, and
notwithstanding his jacket and thick muddy
boots, desired him to be admitted into the
hall, thinking that he would be lost in the
crowd. But to my great astonishment, the
moment I made my appearance on the stage,
I spied the cabman directly facing me, who
was creating a great sensation by the contrast
of features and apparel with the lovely
countenances and rich toilettes of the ladies
seated in the front rows.

"All the pieces I executed were applauded
with enthusiasm. I obtained a signal success,
but the man in the jacket was at least as
triumphant as myself. He clapped his hands
and shouted in the middle of a passage when
everybody else was silent. His gesticulations
and applauses, which partook of delirium, as
much as his burlesque appearance, attracted
the attention of the whole company.

"On the following morning, when I rose, I
was informed that a man was in waiting without,
who desired an interview with me; he would
not send in his name, and as I did not choose
to hurry myself for his sake, my attention
was suddenly excited by the unceremonious
appearance of the identical individual who
had created so much stir in the concert-room.
My first impulse was to throw him over the
banisters, but his demeanour was so humble,
that any incipient anger soon subsided.

"'Diavolo! What do you want?'

"'Excellency!' replied he, 'I come to solicit a favour of you; a very great favour. I am father of four children, and have the honour to be your fellow-countryman. You are wealthy; your fame is unequalled; and, if you please, you can *make my fortune*'!

"'What do you mean?'

"'Well! authorise me to write in large letters at the back of my vehicle these two words:—"PAGANINI'S CAB!"'

"I assented. The poor fellow threw himself at my feet, declaring himself the happiest man alive. He was right: six months afterwards I found him at Florence, in the enjoyment of a comfortable income, derived solely from the designation of his cab, and his musical repute at Vienna!"

Economy Paganini.

Before Paganini left London for Dublin, he had a grand "set to" with his washer-woman, in consequence of her having charged him fourpence *half-penny* for washing his shirt, when a laundress at Dover, who washed him a couple upon his arrival at that port, charged him only *fourpence*. "How de devil is dis?" exclaimed the enraged musician: de woman at Dovare only charged me *four pennies*; and you charge me four pennies, and one half-penny *more* dan dat! How is all dis, I ask of you?" The affrighted washerwoman, half petrified at the violent gestures of the Signor, stated, that "four-

pence *half-penny* was the regular charge for
a shirt which was *plaited*." "Den I tell you
what, woman," vociferated the *poor* Italian,
"Gote d—n the plaits, I will have none of
dem! den I shall pay you but *four* pennies,
and dat is quite enough!" So saying, the
Signor paid the bill, after making a deduction
from the amount, of one half-penny per shirt!
Paganini is said to have realised between
£16,000 and £17,000 in England.

Anecdote of Nicolo Paganini.

In the year 1817, when Paganini was at
Verona, Valdalrini, a very skilful violinist,
and leader of the orchestra at the great
theatre of that town, jealous of the applause
which Paganini obtained upon every night
of his performance, reviled him as a charlatan,
and said, that however he might excel in
some pieces of his own particular *repertorium*,
yet there was a certain *concerto* of his
(Valdalrini's) composition which he would
be incapable of executing. Paganini upon
hearing this, informs Valdalrini immediately
of his resolution to perform his composition.
This trial of skill, which was a powerful
attraction held out to the public, he wired
to reserve for his last concert. The day of
rehearsal is appointed, Paganini fails not
to attend, not so much to prepare himself,
as to comply with the established custom,
the music which he executes upon the
occasion is not that which he proposes to

perform; but according to his custom, he improvisates on the orchestral movements, and intersperses, by way of filling up, a multitude of delicious passages which his imagination produces with an almost incredible impulse.

The rehearsal resembles more a prefatory concert, which leaves on the minds of all present an unexpected foretaste of the wonders of the representation to come. With Paganini one must almost always expect a surprise of this sort; the musicians called to accompany him are so disconcerted, that their instruments escape from them in their astonishment; they sit amazed, forgetting, in their admiration, the task prescribed to them.

Valdalrini's disappointment on hearing anything but his own music, may easily be conceived; and when Paganini had ceased playing, he approached him and said, "*Mon ami*, that is not my concerto that you have been executing, I absolutely found no one thing of what I wrote." "Do not be uneasy, *mon cher*," replied Paganini, "at the concert you will recognise your work perfectly; I only require of you then a little indulgence." The next day the concert took place. Paganini began by playing several pieces of his own choice, reserving that of Valdalrini to terminate the evening with. Everybody was in the expectation of something extraordinary; some thought he intended changing the

orchestral means and effects; others supposed he would give the theme of Valdalrini's
music, in making to it, in his own way, the
most brilliant additions; none were in the
secret. Paganini appears at length, holding
in his hand a bamboo cane; everybody
enquires what he can intend to do with it.
Suddenly, he seizes his violin, and using
his cane like a bow, he plays the concerto
from one end to the other, which the author
thought impossible to execute without long
and unremitting study. Not only did he
give the most difficult passages, but he
introduced among them the most charming
variations, without ceasing for one moment
to exhibit that grace, that intensity of feeling
and vigour, which characterise his talent.—
La Belle Assemblée, June 1831.

Paganini robbed at Cheltenham.

The Cheltenham correspondent of the
Morning Chronicle says:

"An untoward incident occurred in the
afternoon of yesterday, which at one time
assumed a rather serious aspect. Paganini,
in advertising his concerts, had stated 'that
his numerous engagements would render it
impossible for him to remain beyond that
time'; yet having engaged to play at the
theatre last night, he was accordingly
announced. This the residents and visitors
of the place considered an act of unfairness

towards the regular Subscription Balls at
the Rotunda, especially as Mr Jearrad, the
proprietor, had relinquished his usual musical
entertainment on the previous evening, in
order that Paganini's talents might have full
scope.   Immediately the Signor's intention
was, therefore, made known, Captain M.
Berkeley and W. L. Lawrence, Esq., took
upon themselves to print a handbill, calling
upon the nobility and gentry to support the
established amusements of the town, by
patronising the ball of last night, considering
it merely as an act of justice to the proprietor.
The effect of this was to secure a thronged
attendance at the Rotunda Ball, and so poor
an assemblage at the theatre, that Paganini
refused to perform.   This was communicated
to the audience by the manager, who
expressed himself *ready to return the
admission money.*   Instead of quietly with-
drawing, they (the audience) proceeded *en
masse* to the Plough Hotel, to demand of
Paganini the fulfilment of his engagement.
Here a formidable mob was soon collected;
and after threatening to pull the house down,
and uttering denunciations against the musical
phenomenon, *succeeded in frightening him into
compliance*; and he went to the theatre, where
he performed two of his most favourite pieces
with his wonted success and *éclat.*   The
performance at the theatre was for playhouse
prices.   The Signor left at midnight, in
a chaise and four, from the Plough, for
London."

Thus it appears that by bodily fear the fiddler was induced to give his labour for a price he deemed inadequate. How does this differ from robbery? we see no distinction. Paganini's performance is his property, and to force it from him by threats and intimidation is as much robbery as to take the purse, which is the price of his performance, on the highway. The Cheltenham rioters doubtless thought they had done a mighty fine thing when they had bullied the unprotected foreigner out of the display of his skill; but if by the same proceeding they had taken notes of another sort they would themselves have had to perform on the one string for the exploit. Where were the magistrates of the place when this riot occurred? When clowns order their own prices by assembling in mobs and threatening violence, they are hung without mercy. We do not know what the distinction is in law which gives the licence of riot and compulsion to the folks of Cheltenham. Paganini may return to the Continent and report that he has been among a people without law or manners.—*New Monthly Magazine*, 1831.

Paganini.

Paganini is indeed a wonderful man: he has performed a feat which no other man in the world could have accomplished—he has put Brougham down. At a dinner at

the Mansion House, the health of the Lord
Chancellor having been given, he rose to
return thanks :—" Feelings overpower me—
proudest moment of my life, and——" were
on his lips. Paganini, entering the room
at the instant, naturally supposed that so
much applause could not be meant for any
one on earth but himself, and to show
instantly how well he deserved it, got upon
a chair and commenced his performance.
Lord Brougham sat down. It is reported
that there were persons so tasteless as to
call for the speech in preference to the fiddle.
As the scene was a city feast, it is not
incredible.—*New Monthly Magazine*, 1831.

Death of Paganini.

This celebrated violinist died at Nice, on
the 29th of May, after a lingering illness.
He has left one son, who inherits a large
fortune. Paganini's remains were embalmed,
to be removed to Genoa, his native town,
for interment. The most wonderful performer
on the violin has been taken from the musical
world. He has hosts of imitators, but not
one rival. He carried execution on the
fiddle beyond any former or subsequent
performer, and his almost demoniac feats
of dexterity were only equalled by his touching tone, beautiful expression, impassioned
feeling, and correct intonation. His compositions partook of his unearthly appearance ;

his style was "sad by fits, by starts was wild."
His "Witches' Dance" was incomparably
grotesque, eccentric, and true withal, and
never did violin weep such strains as his
"Nel cor piu." Paganini was avaricious, and
little to be depended on in worldly affairs;
but some fits of generosity by which he
was impelled have astonished even himself.
He would never, it is said, forgive himself
for the gift of 20,000 francs to Berlitz, whom
he styled the modern Beethoven. He was
engaged in the Casino speculation in Paris,
but took fright and abandoned it; for which
heavy damages were awarded against him,
the payment of which he avoided by his
return to Italy, where he died.

PRINTED AT THE EDINBURGH PRESS
9 AND 11 YOUNG STREET

www.ingramcontent.com/pod-product-compliance
Lightning Source LLC
Chambersburg PA
CBHW020501100426
42813CB00030B/3063/J